how2become.com

Verbal Reasoning Tests

ULTIMATE 2nd Edition

www.How2Become.com

Orders: Please contact How2Become Ltd, Suite 1, 60 Churchill Square Business Centre, Kings Hill, Kent ME19 4YU.

You can order through Amazon.co.uk under ISBN 9781912370634 via the website www.How2Become.com, Gardners or Bertrams.

ISBN: 9781912370634

First published in 2019 by How2Become Ltd.

Copyright © 2019 How2Become.

Typeset for How2Become Ltd by Jacob Senior.

As part of this product you have also received FREE access to online tests that will help you to pass your Verbal Reasoning Tests.

To gain access, simply go to:

www.PsychometricTestsOnline.co.uk

Get more products for passing any test at:

www.How2Become.com

CONTENTS

Introduction 7

Advice for Improving Your Scores 9

Verbal Reasoning Test 1 29

    Answers - Verbal Reasoning Test 1 42

Verbal Reasoning Test 2 55

    Answers - Verbal Reasoning Test 2 69

Verbal Reasoning Test 3 87

    Answers - Verbal Reasoning Test 3 100

Verbal Reasoning Final Mock Exam 111

    Answers - Verbal Reasoning Final Mock Exam 138

500 More Verbal Reasoning Question 163

A Few Final Words 359

INTRODUCTION

Verbal reasoning tests have been in use for many years. They are used as a tool by employers to assess potential employees for specific careers. The most common type of verbal reasoning test in use today is the one that involves a passage of text and a requirement for the candidate to state whether certain statements relating to the passage are: true, false, or cannot say from the information provided.

Verbal reasoning tests are usually timed, and as such we recommend you carry out lots of practice under strict timed conditions. It is extremely difficult to replicate exact testing conditions during preparation; however, by preparing yourself in this manner you will be giving yourself the best chance of success. The time limit supplied in the majority of verbal reasoning tests is designed so that you will find it impossible to complete the test. Those candidates who are unaware of this fact will often panic as they see the clock ticking away, yet their progress through the test does not match the quantity of time remaining. Yes, it is important to work as fast as you can, but accuracy is also an essential element of your overall score. Tests are now far more advanced and sophisticated than they used to be. They give an accurate assessment of how a potential employee is likely to perform in a certain role.

The assessor/employer will get to see exactly how many questions you attempted, how many you got right and also how many you scored incorrectly. Within this workbook, we will avoid advising you to 'guess' the final few questions if you notice that you only have a few seconds left at the end. Some assessors will deduct marks for guessing or incorrect answers. Therefore, it is important that we concentrate on both speed and accuracy during this workbook.

Advice for Improving Your Scores

Develop an Action Plan

When preparing for your verbal reasoning tests implement an action plan of preparation. We recommend carrying out at least 30 minutes practice per day/evening in the fortnight before the test. The reason why we state a fortnight is simply because this is an approximate amount of time that the employer will give you to prepare before your test date. If you get longer to prepare, use the time wisely.

Time Yourself From the Outset

Prepare for the tests by using 'time' from the outset. This means timing yourself even when carrying out practice tests. Get used to the feeling of the clock ticking down and the pressure you will be under. Many people do not carry out practice tests under timed conditions. When it comes to the real test day they suffer as a result. It is also important to be aware that you should time yourself from the point that you start reading the verbal comprehension passage. Some people believe that the test only starts when you study the answer options; this is incorrect.

Have an Organised Mindset

Develop an organised mindset. There is a difference between a 'seasoned' test taker and a novice test taker. A seasoned test taker will approach the test in a formalised manner, whereas the novice will bluff their way through the test. Your approach to verbal reasoning tests should include the following:

1. The only way to gain high scores is to ensure that your mind and body are at their best. In the fortnight before the test avoid alcohol, cigarettes, coffee and junk food. Make a conscious effort to eat healthily, drink plenty of water and get plenty of sleep/rest.

2. A large percentage of test takers fail to follow the instructions provided at the commencement of the test. Listen to what the test administrator tells you. Most candidates are more concerned about the other test takers in the room rather than being concerned about the rules of the test. Focus on your own performance only and do not worry about anyone else in the room. Listen to what is being said and follow all instructions carefully. If you are unsure, ask.

Accurate Marking is Crucial

The vast majority of verbal reasoning tests are multiple-choice in nature. The main reason for this type of test is because it allows the employer/ assessor to score a large number of tests quickly. Because of this fact it is essential that you complete the marking sheet accurately. If you miss a question be sure to leave a space on the marking sheet. People will occasionally fail an entire test because they failed to leave a space on the marking sheet after missing out a question.

Pace Yourself According to the Allocated Time

Just before the test commences the test administrator will inform you of how many questions there are within the test and also the time limit you have to complete it. This is your opportunity to provide yourself with an 'approximate' time to answer each question. For example, if you are informed that there are thirty questions in the test and you have twenty minutes to complete them, this gives you an average of forty seconds per question. If you find yourself spending up to two minutes on a question then you are probably spending far too much time trying to answer it.

Concentrate Fully

During the test concentrate fully on the passage of text you are reading. It is pointless reading the passage unless you are concentrating fully on the content. It is very easy to get distracted, either by other test takers or by worrying about the remaining time.

Use an Approach that Suits You

The vast majority of people who take verbal reasoning tests approach them by reading the entire passage through once before turning to the questions. Try reading the question first and then scan the passage for 'keywords' and 'phrases' which match the question. The bottom line is this: there are no hard and fast rules for approaching the questions. Choose a method that works for you. We can guarantee you that you will have developed your own method for answering the questions by the time you have completed this workbook.

Answer the questions based solely on the information provided. Candidates who sit verbal reasoning tests often fall into the trap of answering the question based on fact, rather than answering the question based solely on the information provided in the text. The type of question you are likely to encounter will involve a passage of text followed by a series of questions which must be answered either TRUE, FALSE, or CANNOT SAY based on the information given.

Here's an example of how people fall foul of the CANNOT SAY option:

Read the following text before answering the question as either TRUE, FALSE or CANNOT SAY based on the information provided.

> A uniform is a set of standard clothing worn by members of an organisation whilst participating in that organisation's activity. Modern uniforms are worn by armed forces and paramilitary organisations such as; police, emergency services and security guards, in some workplaces and schools and by inmates in prisons. In some countries, officials also wear uniforms in some of their duties; such is the case of the Commissioned Corps of the United States Public Health Service or the French Prefects.

Q. Police officers are required to wear a uniform.

The answer to the question is CANNOT SAY based on the information provided. Many candidates will answer this question as TRUE; simply because we all know that police officers do in fact wear a uniform. Crucially, the word 'required' is not mentioned in the passage. The important lesson here is to only answer the question based solely on the information provided, regardless of what you know to be fact.

Here's a quick refresher on what is meant by TRUE, FALSE, and CANNOT SAY in the context of the Verbal Reasoning test.

TRUE - If a statement is 'true', then it can be verified by the text. This means that the text must explicitly or implicitly mention something which proves the statement to be correct. In other words, you cannot make any assumptions about the text. There must either be direct evidence for the statement, or a strong inference to support the statement.

FALSE - If a statement is 'false', there must be evidence in the text which contradicts the statement. For example, if the question statement says 'all swans are white', but the text says 'there is such a thing as a black swan', then the statement is false because it is directly contradicted by the text.

CANNOT SAY - If there is not enough evidence to verify that the statement is true or false, then the correct answer is 'cannot say' Simply put, this means that you cannot say the statement is true or false based on the information provided in the passage.

A Sample Verbal Reasoning Test Question and How to Approach It

Let's now take a look at a sample verbal reasoning test question in a format which is common amongst employers nowadays.

You will normally find a passage of text which is followed by a number of questions. Following the questions, you are required to state whether the questions are TRUE, FALSE, or CANNOT SAY without further information.

Read the following text before answering the questions as either TRUE, FALSE or CANNOT SAY from the information given.

Basic Holiday Rights for Employees

There is a minimum right to paid holiday, but your employer may offer more than this. All employees are entitled to a minimum of 5.6 weeks paid leave per year. Those employees who work for five days a week are entitled to 28 days per year annual leave (capped at a statutory maximum of 28 days for all working patterns). Employees who work part-time are entitled to the same level of holiday pro rata (5.6 times your normal working week) e.g. 16.8 days for someone working three days a week. All employees will start building up holiday entitlement as soon as they start work with the employer.

The employer has the right to control when you take your holiday but you must get paid the same level of pay whilst on holiday. When you finish working for an employer you get paid for any holiday you have not taken. The employer may include bank and public holidays in your minimum entitlement.

You continue to be entitled to your holiday leave throughout any additional maternity/paternity leave and adoption leave.

1. An employer may not offer you more than the minimum paid holiday.

2. In addition to paternity leave you are entitled to your normal holiday.

3. All employees only start building up holiday leave 5.6 weeks after commencement of employment.

4. Employees who receive more than the minimum holiday entitlement are often grateful to their employer.

The above sample question consists of a passage of text which relates to basic holiday rights for employees followed by four questions. You have to state whether the questions are either TRUE, FALSE or CANNOT SAY from the information given. The important thing to remember is that you should solely base your answers on the passage of text provided. Let's break each question down individually:

1. An employer may not offer you more than the minimum paid holiday.

By reading the passage carefully you will note that the following sentence relates to Question 1:

"There is a minimum right to paid holiday, but your employer may offer more than this."

We can deduce from the passage that Question 1 is in fact FALSE, simply because an employer may offer more than the minimum paid holiday.

Fortunately for us, the first question related to the very first sentence in the passage. However, in the majority of cases this will not be the norm.

2. In addition to paternity leave you are entitled to your normal holiday.

By reading the passage carefully you will note that the following sentence relates to Question 2:

"You continue to be entitled to your holiday leave throughout any additional maternity/paternity leave and adoption leave."

We can deduce from the passage that Question 2 is in fact TRUE. An employee is entitled to their holiday leave throughout paternity leave.

Question 2 is a very good example of how 'scanning' the passage can save you time. You will note that the word 'paternity' is only used once throughout the entire passage. By scanning the passage quickly in search of specific keywords or phrases you will be able to reach the section of the passage that relates to the question and thus answer the question far quicker than reading the entire passage. Once again, there is no right or wrong way for answering the questions; choose a method which works for you.

3. All employees only start building up holiday leave 5.6 weeks after commencement of employment.

By reading the passage carefully you will note that the following sentence relates to Question 3:

"All employees will start building up holiday entitlement as soon as they start work with the employer."

We can deduce from the passage that Question 3 is in fact false based on the information provided. An employee starts building up holiday as soon as they start work with the employer, not 5.6 weeks after commencement of employment.

4. Employees who receive more than the minimum holiday entitlement are often grateful to their employer.

By reading the passage carefully you will note that none of the content relates to the question. At no point does it state that employees who receive more than the minimum holiday entitlement are often grateful to their employer, or otherwise. Therefore, the answer is CANNOT SAY based on the information provided. Although it is probably true in real life that most employees would be grateful for receiving more than the minimum holiday requirement, we can only answer the question based solely on the information provided in the passage.

Now try the following five sample questions. Take your time when answering the question as there is no time limit for these specific questions. The answers/explanations are provided following each question.

Read the following text before answering the questions as either TRUE, FALSE or CANNOT SAY from the information given.

WINTER FUEL PAYMENTS

Members of the public may get a winter Fuel Payment if they have reached the qualifying age (born on or before 5 January 1951) and they also normally live in Great Britain or Northern Ireland on any day in the week of 19–25 September 2011. They won't qualify for a Winter Fuel Payment if, throughout the week of 19–25 September 2011, they were in hospital or a care home for more than 52 weeks previously, getting free treatment as an in-patient.

They will also not qualify if they were in custody serving a court sentence, were subject to immigration control and did not qualify for help from the Department for work and Pensions, lived in a care home, an independent hospital, received income-based Jobseeker's Allowance or income-related Employment and Support Allowance.

In addition to these restrictions you cannot qualify for a Winter Fuel Payment if you move to another European Economic Area country or Switzerland.

Winter Fuel Payment is paid for the household and will be paid directly into your bank account or by cheque depending on which format you requested.

Q1a. You can qualify for a Winter Fuel Payment if you move to France.

A - TRUE	B - FALSE	C - CANNOT SAY

Q1b. Winter Fuel Payment can only be paid directly in your bank account.

A - TRUE	B - FALSE	C - CANNOT SAY

Q1c. Members of the public will not qualify for a Winter Fuel Payment if, throughout the week of 19–25 September 2011, they were in a care home.

A - TRUE	B - FALSE	C - CANNOT SAY

Review Your Answers

WINTER FUEL PAYMENTS

Members of the public may get a winter Fuel Payment if they have reached the qualifying age (born on or before 5 January 1951) and they also normally live in Great Britain or Northern Ireland on any day in the week of 19–25 September 2011. They won't qualify for a Winter Fuel Payment if, throughout the week of 19–25 September 2011, they were in hospital or a care home for more than 52 weeks previously, getting free treatment as an in-patient.

[c]: They will also not qualify if they were in custody serving a court sentence, were subject to immigration control and did not qualify for help from the Department for Work and Pensions, lived in a care home, an independent hospital, received income-based Jobseeker's Allowance or income-related Employment and Support Allowance.

In addition to these restrictions [a]: you cannot qualify for a Winter Fuel Payment if you move to another European Economic Area country or Switzerland.

[b]: Winter Fuel Payment is paid for the household and will be paid directly into your bank account or by cheque depending on which format you requested.

Q1a. You can qualify for a Winter Fuel Payment if you move to France.

Answer - B (FALSE)

The passage states "you cannot qualify for a Winter Fuel Payment if you move to another European Economic Area country". The statement is, therefore, false.

Q1b. Winter Fuel Payment can only be paid directly in your bank account.

Answer - B (FALSE)

The statement is false because the passage states "Winter Fuel Payment is paid for the household and will be paid directly into your bank account or by cheque depending on which format you requested".

Q1c. Members of the public will not qualify for a winter Fuel Payment if, throughout the week of 19–25 September 2011, they were in a care home.

Answer - A (TRUE)

The passage confirms the statement to be true.

ANIMAL EUTHANASIA

Animal euthanasia is the practice of terminating the life of an animal in a painless or minimally painful way in order to stop suffering or other undesired conditions in life.

This may be voluntary or involuntary, and carried out with or without a physician. In a medical environment, this can be carried out by oral, intravenous or intramuscular drug administration. Laws around the world vary greatly with regard to animal euthanasia and are constantly subject to change as cultural values shift and better palliative care or treatments become available. Reasons for animal euthanasia include:

· Terminal illness – e.g. cancer.

· Rabies.

· Behavioural problems (that usually cannot be corrected) – e.g. aggression.

· Illness or broken limbs that would cause suffering for the animal to live with, or when the owner cannot afford (or has a moral objection to) treatment.

· Old age – Deterioration to loss of major bodily functions. Severe impairment of the quality of life.

· Lack of homes – Some shelters receive considerably more sur- rendered animals than they are capable of re-housing. This may be attributed to irresponsible owners who do not spay or neuter pets, causing unwanted litters. Some pets turned in to animal shelters are not adopted out.

Q2a. Shifts in cultural values are the main causes for changes in the law around the world in relation to animal euthanasia.

A - TRUE	B - FALSE	C - CANNOT SAY

Q2b. Animal testing is cruel and immoral.

A - TRUE	B - FALSE	C - CANNOT SAY

Q2c. Irresponsible owners who do not spay or neuter pets may be the cause of some shelters receiving more surrendered animals than they are capable of re-housing.

A - TRUE	B - FALSE	C - CANNOT SAY

Review Your Answers

Q2a. Shifts in cultural values are the main causes for changes in the law around the world in relation to animal euthanasia.

Answer - C (CANNOT SAY)

The passage does not state that shifts in cultural values are the main causes for changes in the law. Therefore, we cannot say from the information provided.

Q2b. Animal testing is cruel and immoral.

Answer - C (CANNOT SAY)

The passage does not provide any information relating to this statement. The correct answer is therefore cannot say.

Q2c. Irresponsible owners who do not spay or neuter pets may be the cause of some shelters receiving more surrendered animals than they are capable of re-housing.

Answer - A (TRUE)

The passage confirms that this statement is true.

WHITEHAM SUPERMARKET

Barry and Bill work at their local supermarket in the town of Whiteham. Barry works every day except Wednesday.

The supermarket is run by Barry's brother Elliot who is married to Sarah. Sarah and Elliot have two children called Marcus and Michelle who are both seven-years-old and they live in the road adjacent to the supermarket.

Barry lives in a town called Redford, which is seven miles from Whiteham. Bill's girlfriend, Maria, works in a factory in her hometown of Brownhaven.

The town of Redford is four miles from Whiteham and six miles from the seaside town of Tenford. Sarah and Elliot take their children on holiday to Tenford twice a year and Barry usually gives them a lift in his car. Barry's mum lives in Tenford and he tries to visit her once a week at 2pm when he is not working.

Q3a. Brownhaven is seven miles from Whiteham.

A - TRUE	B - FALSE	C - CANNOT SAY

Q3b. Barry works at the local supermarket on Sundays.

A - TRUE	B - FALSE	C - CANNOT SAY

Q3c. The town of Redford is four miles from the town of Tenford.

A - TRUE	B - FALSE	C - CANNOT SAY

WHITEHAM SUPERMARKET

Barry and Bill work at their local supermarket in the town of Whiteham. [b]:Barry works every day except Wednesday.

The supermarket is run by Barry's brother Elliot who is married to Sarah. Sarah and Elliot have two children called Marcus and Michelle who are both seven-years-old and they live in the road adjacent to the supermarket.

Barry lives in a town called Redford, which is seven miles from Whiteham. Bill's girlfriend, Maria, works in a factory in her hometown of Brownhaven.

The town of Redford is four miles from Whiteham and six miles from the seaside town of Tenford. Sarah and Elliot take their children on holiday to Tenford twice a year and Barry usually gives them a lift in his car. Barry's mum lives in Tenford and he tries to visit her once a week at 2pm when he is not working.

Review Your Answers

3. Read the following text before answering the questions as either TRUE, FALSE or CANNOT SAY from the information given.

Q3a. Brownhaven is seven miles from Whiteham.

Answer - C (CANNOT SAY)

Based on the information provided in the passage we cannot say whether this statement is true or false.

Q3b. Barry works at the local supermarket on Sundays.

Answer - A (TRUE)

The passage confirms that "Barry works every day except Wednesday." The statement is, therefore, true.

Q3c. The town of Redford is four miles from the town of Tenford.

Answer - B (FALSE)

The passage states that "The town of Redford is four miles from Whiteham and six miles from the seaside town of Tenford." The statement is, therefore, false based on the information provided.

NATIONAL INSURANCE CONTRIBUTIONS

People pay National Insurance contributions in order to build up their entitlement to a state pension and other social security benefits.

The amount that you pay is directly linked to the amount you earn. If you earn over a certain amount, your employer deducts Class 1 National Insurance contributions from your wages through the PAYE system.

You pay a lower rate of National Insurance contributions if you're a member of your employer's 'contracted-out' pension scheme, or you're a married woman – or widow – who holds a valid 'election certificate'.

Your employer also pays employer National Insurance contributions based on your earnings and on any benefits you get with your job, for example a company car. HMRC keeps track of your contributions through your National Insurance number. This is like an account number and is unique to you.

Q4a. People pay National Insurance contributions in order to build up housing benefits.

A - TRUE	B - FALSE	C - CANNOT SAY

Q4b. HMRC stands for 'Her Majesty's Revenue and Customs'.

A - TRUE	B - FALSE	C - CANNOT SAY

Q4c. An employer pays employer National Insurance contributions if an employee has a company car.

A - TRUE	B - FALSE	C - CANNOT SAY

NATIONAL INSURANCE CONTRIBUTIONS

People pay National Insurance contributions in order to build up their entitlement to a state pension and other social security benefits.

The amount that you pay is directly linked to the amount you earn. If you earn over a certain amount, your employer deducts Class 1 National Insurance contributions from your wages through the PAYE system.

You pay a lower rate of National Insurance contributions if you're a member of your employer's 'contracted-out' pension scheme, or you're a married woman – or widow – who holds a valid 'election certificate'.

^cYour employer also pays employer National Insurance contributions based on your earnings and on any benefits you get with your job, for example a company car. HMRC keeps track of your contributions through your National Insurance number. This is like an account number and is unique to you.

Review Your Answers

Q4a. People pay National Insurance contributions in order to build up housing benefits.

Answer - C (CANNOT SAY)

Although the statement makes reference to social security benefits, it does not confirm that these include housing benefits. The correct answer is cannot say based on the information provided.

Q4b. HMRC stands for 'Her Majesty's Revenue and Customs'.

Answer - C (CANNOT SAY)

The passage makes no reference to this fact; therefore, the correct answer is cannot say based on the information provided.

Q4c. An employer pays employer National Insurance contributions if an employee has a company car.

Answer - A (TRUE)

The passage states that "Your employer also pays employer National Insurance contributions based on your earnings and on any benefits you get with your job, for example a company car". The statement is true.

FAMILY HOLIDAY

Janet and Steve have been married for twenty-seven years. They have a daughter called Jessica who is twenty-five-years-old. They all want to go on holiday together but cannot make up their minds on where to go.

Janet's first choice would be somewhere hot and sunny abroad. Her second choice would be somewhere in their home country that involves a sporting activity. She does not like hill-climbing or walking holidays but her third choice would be a skiing holiday.

Steve's first choice would be a walking holiday in the hills somewhere in their home country and his second choice would be a sunny holiday abroad. He does not enjoy skiing. Jessica's first choice would be a skiing holiday and her second choice would be a sunny holiday abroad. Jessica's third choice would be a walking holiday in the hills of their home country.

Q5a. Jessica's first choice would be a walking holiday in the hills of their home country.

A - TRUE	B - FALSE	C - CANNOT SAY

Q5b. Janet and Jessica have been married for twenty-seven years.

A - TRUE	B - FALSE	C - CANNOT SAY

Q5c. Jessica would rather go skiing than go on a sunny holiday abroad.

A - TRUE	B - FALSE	C - CANNOT SAY

Review Your Answers

FAMILY HOLIDAY

[b]: Janet and Steve have been married for twenty-seven years. They have a daughter called Jessica who is twenty-five-years-old. They all want to go on holiday together but cannot make up their minds on where to go.

Janet's first choice would be somewhere hot and sunny abroad. Her second choice would be somewhere in their home country that involves a sporting activity. She does not like hill-climbing or walking holidays but her third choice would be a skiing holiday.

[a & c]: Steve's first choice would be a walking holiday in the hills some- where in their home country and his second choice would be a sunny holiday abroad. He does not enjoy skiing. Jessica's first choice would be a skiing holiday and her second choice would be a sunny holiday abroad. Jessica's third choice would be a walking holiday in the hills of their home country.

Q5a. Jessica's first choice would be a walking holiday in the hills of their home country.

Answer - B (FALSE)

The passage states that Jessica's first choice would be a skiing holiday; therefore, the sentence is false.

Q5b. Janet and Jessica have been married for twenty-seven years.

Answer - B (FALSE)

The sentence states that Janet and Jessica have been married, whereas the passage states Janet and Steve. Therefore, the sentence is false.

Q5c. Jessica would rather go skiing than go on a sunny holiday abroad.

Answer - A (TRUE)

We can tell from the sentence that Jessica would rather go skiing than go on a sunny holiday abroad as skiing is her first choice. The correct answer is true.

Following the five sample questions you should have a better understanding of how the questions are formatted and also how to approach them. You will have gathered that the most important factor when answering the questions is to totally base your answer on the facts that are provided within the passage.

INSIDER TIPS AND ADVICE FOR PASSING THE VERBAL REASONING TEST

Before you try your first timed test we want to provide you with a number of crucial tips that will give you a better insight into verbal reasoning tests and how you can go about improving your scores.

Tip 1: Don't aim for a set mark, aim to do the best you can.

Many people ask what the scoring criteria is for verbal reasoning tests. They want to know how many they need to get correct in order to pass. To be honest, every employer/test administrator will have a different standard. Tests of this nature in the public sector normally require a pass rate of 70%. Our advice would be to not focus on the pass mark but instead focus on trying to get every question correct. Some employers will set the pass mark according to the overall average score amongst the applicants. Therefore, it is pointless worrying about the pass mark.

Tip 2: Practise against the clock.

The vast majority of verbal reasoning tests are timed; therefore, you need to practise under timed conditions. Savvy test takers will be fully aware of the amount of time they have to answer each question on average. We encourage you to do the same during your preparation.

Tip 3: Listen to the test administrator.

Test administrators should be suitably qualified in order to administer the test. They will provide you with sufficient information on how to take the test and the rules/guidelines involved immediately prior to the real test. This is also your opportunity to ask any questions that you may have. In the majority of cases you will be given the opportunity to try a small number of sample questions.

Tip 4: Don't let the 'odd one out' catch you out.

Be prepared to face a variety of test styles. The verbal reasoning test that you are required to undertake should be representative of the type of role you are applying for. That is why you do not see many verbal reasoning tests that require you to 'select the odd one out' or 'fill in the missing words' of a sentence, simply because the majority of occupational roles are not relevant to this type of test.

Tip 5: Keep focused on the test.

You should learn to concentrate intently on the test you are taking and the questions you are required to answer. You should learn to block everything that is irrelevant to the test out of your mind. That means not worrying about what the other test takers are doing or where they are in relation to you in the test! Focus on your own test only.

Tip 6: Preparation also includes rest and the right diet.

The chances are, you won't be able to rest fully the night before your test. Our advice is to get plenty of rest in the fortnight before the test. Eat healthily, get some exercise (brisk walking is perfect) and avoid coffee and alcohol too. Energy drinks may claim to increase stimulation and concentration, but how long for is debatable. The danger is, once the effect wears off, you will start to feel lethargic. Choose clean, healthy water instead.

Tip 7: Obey the test administrator.

Test administrators are required to keep a log of events during the test. They are required to write down any incidents that occur, such as noise in neighbouring rooms or interruptions that may occur. They are also required to write down any anomalies that occur with the test takers. Any information that is written down could be used to influence your scores, both good and bad. Follow all instructions carefully and stop writing when told to do so!

Tip 8: Be prepared to say 'cannot say'.

As part of your interview skills preparation you're taught to always have something to say in response to a question. You never answer with "don't know" or "can't say", instead you always seek to find a relevant response which will put you in a good light. So, for many test takers it is unnerving to answer with the option 'cannot say'. In fact, this is often the reason some companies use this specific abbreviation – to test your nerve. So, it is important to remember that 'cannot say' is only an abbreviation of the 'cannot say on the information provided' option and is a valid answer from observant and successful candidates.

The next element of your preparation is to include 'time'. We are now going to provide you with your first timed test. The test that follows consists of ten sample tests and you have ten minutes in which to complete them. You will note that you have an average of sixty seconds per question. As per our previous advice, if you find that you are spending well over the average time allocation on a particular question, you should move on to the next one.

If you complete the test within the allotted time, go back over any questions you were unsure of and thoroughly check them.

Please use a pencil to circle your chosen answers. We also recommend that you have a stopwatch or clock with you so that you can keep a check on the time.

When you are ready, turn the page and begin. The answers and explanations are provided at the end of the test.

VERBAL REASONING TEST 1

During Verbal Reasoning Test 1 there are 10 practice passages which each contain 3 questions. Answer each question based solely on the information provided. You must select either TRUE, FALSE or CANNOT SAY based on the information provided in the passage.

- You have 10 minutes to complete the test.

- Concentrate fully on each test.

- If unsure of an answer you should select the one that you believe to be correct.

- Avoid all forms of wild guessing.

Once you have completed the test check your answers with the ones that are provided.

VERBAL REASONING TEST 1

Number of Passages = 10

Questions per Passage = 3

Total Number of Questions = 30

Surname:

Forename:

Date of Test (dd/mm/yyyy):

Allotted Time = 10 Minutes

For the following questions, read the text before answering the questions as either TRUE, FALSE or CANNOT SAY from the information given.

ANALYSTS PROVE FORECASTERS WRONG

The Office for National Statistics (ONS) said internet shopping and sales of household goods had been better in October compared with previous months. However, sales of clothing and footwear, where many retailers cut prices before Christmas, were particularly weak.

The increase came as a surprise to many analysts who were predicting a 0.4% fall in internet shopping and sales of household goods. The rise meant that retail sale volumes in the three months leading up to January were up by 2.6% on the previous quarter. The final quarter of the year is a better guide to the underlying trend than one month's figures.

Some analysts cautioned that the heavy seasonal adjustment of the raw spending figures at the turn of the year made interpreting the data difficult. Even so, the government will be relieved that spending appears to be holding up despite the squeeze on incomes caused by high inflation, rising unemployment, a weak housing market and the crisis in the eurozone.

Retail sales account for less than half of total consumer spending and do not include the purchase of cars or eating out. The ONS said that its measure of inflation in the high street – the annual retail sales deflator – fell to 2.2% last month, its lowest level since November 2009. Ministers are hoping that lower inflation will boost real income growth during the course of 2012.

Q1a. Ministers hope that higher inflation will boost real income growth during 2012.

A - TRUE	B - FALSE	C - CANNOT SAY

Q1b. Analysts predicted a 0.4% rise in the sales of household goods.

A - TRUE	B - FALSE	C - CANNOT SAY

Q1c. The crisis in the eurozone is contributing to the squeeze on incomes.

A - TRUE	B - FALSE	C - CANNOT SAY

LONG-SERVICE PAYMENTS

Employees who attain fifteen years' continuous service between 7th November 2003 and 30th June 2007 shall qualify for the long-service payment at the rate applicable at the time. Employees who are promoted to a higher role during this period will cease to qualify for the payment but will receive a minimum pay increase on promotion of £300 per annum, which will be achieved through partial protection of the long-service payment.

Where the pay assimilation process on 7th November 2003 created a basic pay increase of more than 7%, and the employee was in receipt of the long-service payment, the payment has been reduced with effect from that date by the amount that the increase exceeded 7%. The consequent pay rates were set out in circular NJC/01/04.

PAY PROTECTION FOR EMPLOYEES ON THE RETAINED DUTY SYSTEM

Where an employee on the retained duty system has not received a pay increase of at least 7% (for the same pattern and level of activity) following full implementation of the pay award effective from 7th November 2003, the fire and rescue authority may introduce arrangements to ensure that such an increase is achieved.

Q2a. If an employee who is on the retained duty system has not received a pay increase of at least 7% following the implementation of the pay award, the fire and rescue service must introduce arrangements to ensure that such an increase is achieved.

A - TRUE	B - FALSE	C - CANNOT SAY

Q2b. Employees who attain fifteen years' continuous service between 7th November 2003 and 30th June 2008 shall qualify for the long-service payment at the rate applicable at the time.

A - TRUE	B - FALSE	C - CANNOT SAY

Q2c. The pay assimilation process on 7th November 2003 created a basic pay increase for all employees of more than 7%.

A - TRUE	B - FALSE	C - CANNOT SAY

DATA WAREHOUSES

A data warehouse is the main source of information for an organisation's historical data. Its historical data is often referred to as its corporate memory. As an example of how a data warehouse can be put to good use, an organisation would use the information stored in its data warehouse to find out how many particular stock items they sold on a particular day in a particular year. They could also ascertain which employees were off sick on any given day or any given year. The data stored within the warehouse contains essential information so that managers can make appropriate management decisions.

A data warehouse is normally large in size as the information stored usually focuses on basic, structured and organised data. Some of the characteristics of the data in a data warehouse are as follows:

Time-variant - changes to the data in the database are tracked and recorded so that reports can be produced showing changes over time;

Non-volatile - the data in the database is never over-written or deleted but is retained for future reporting;

Integrated - the database contains data from most or all of an organisation's operational applications. This data is useful and meaningful for further processing and analysis.

Q3a. Integrated and non-volatile data form some of the characteristics of a data warehouse.

A - TRUE	B - FALSE	C - CANNOT SAY

Q3b. It is not possible to identify which employees were on sick leave from the information stored in a data warehouse.

A - TRUE	B - FALSE	C - CANNOT SAY

Q3c. Corporate memory is an alternative name given to historical data.

A - TRUE	B - FALSE	C - CANNOT SAY

THE IMPORTANCE OF HEALTH AND SAFETY IN THE WORKPLACE

Employers must protect the health and safety of everyone in your workplace, including people with disabilities, and provide welfare facilities for your employees.

Basic things you need to consider are outlined below.

WELFARE FACILITIES

For your employees' well-being you need to provide:

- Toilets and hand basins, with soap and towels or a hand-dryer, drinking water.

- A place to store clothing (and somewhere to change if special clothing is worn for work).

- Somewhere to rest and eat meals.

HEALTH ISSUES

To have a healthy working environment, make sure there is:

- Good ventilation – a supply of fresh, clean air drawn from outside or a ventilation system.

- A reasonable working temperature (usually at least 16°C, or 13°C for strenuous work, unless other laws require lower temperatures).

- Lighting suitable for the work being carried out.

- Enough room space and suitable workstations and seating.

- A clean workplace with appropriate waste containers.

Q4a. It is the responsibility of the employee for keeping a workplace safe.

A - TRUE	B - FALSE	C - CANNOT SAY

Q4b. Providing the employee with a suitable workstation is a consideration for the employer when making the workplace safe.

A - TRUE	B - FALSE	C - CANNOT SAY

Q4c. An employer must ensure that all floor surfaces are non-slip in order to prevent slips, trips and falls.

A - TRUE	B - FALSE	C - CANNOT SAY

MAGISTRATE TRAINING

The entire selection process for becoming a magistrate can take approximately 12 months, sometimes longer depending on the area.

Once you have been accepted you will be required to undertake a comprehensive training course which is usually held over a 3-day period (18 hours). During this course you will learn the necessary skills that are required in order to become a magistrate.

The training is normally carried out by the Justice Clerk who is responsible for the court. He/she will usually be the legal advisor during your magistrate sittings. They will help you to develop all the necessary skills required in order to carry out your duties professionally and competently.

You will carry out your training as part of a group with other people who have been recruited at the same time as you. This is extremely beneficial as it will allow you to learn in a safe environment.

Training will be given using a variety of methods, which may include pre- course reading, small-group work, use of case studies, computer-based training and CCTV. It is recognised that magistrates are volunteers and that their time is valuable, so every effort is made to provide all training at times and places convenient to trainees. The Ministry of Justice booklet 'Serving as a Magistrate' has more information about the magistracy and the role of magistrates.

Q5a. The comprehensive training course for becoming a magistrate usually consists of 3 days, divided into 6 hours training per day.

A - TRUE	B - FALSE	C - CANNOT SAY

Q5b. An applicant can find out more about the role of a magistrate by reading the Ministry of Justice booklet 'Serving as a Magistrate'.

A - TRUE	B - FALSE	C - CANNOT SAY

Q5c. The selection process for becoming a magistrate will take no longer than 12 months.

A - TRUE	B - FALSE	C - CANNOT SAY

HOW TO ENROL IN OUR ONLINE SELLERS' PROGRAMME

To enrol in our online sellers' programme, you must have an email account, access to the Internet, have a UK distribution facility and also hold the full UK distribution rights to the item(s) you want to sell.

You must have a UK bank account capable of receiving payments via electronic bank transfer (BACS), as this is the only method of payment we offer. Each product you wish to sell in our programme must meet our minimum eligibility standards. These standards relate to quality, value, subject matter, production standards and compliance with intellectual property laws. We reserve the right to remove any products if they do not meet our standards. You are not permitted to sell any products that are deemed to be pornographic or racist.

Any books that you wish to sell via our sellers' programme must have a 10 or 13-digit ISBN number and applicable barcode printed on the back of the book in the bottom right-hand corner.

The barcode must scan to match the ISBN of the book. If the item you want to sell is a music CD then the CD must be in a protective case which meets the relevant British Standard.

The title and artist name must be printed on and readable from the spine (the thin side of the CD). Once again, the CD must contain a barcode which must scan to match the EAN or UPC.

If your item is a DVD or VHS video. Rules that apply to music CDs are also applicable to DVD products.

Q6a. The barcode on a CD must be printed on the back in the bottom right-hand corner.

A - TRUE	B - FALSE	C - CANNOT SAY

Q6b. Pornographic products are permitted in the online sellers' programme.

A - TRUE	B - FALSE	C - CANNOT SAY

Q6c. ISBN is short for International Standard Book Number.

A - TRUE	B - FALSE	C - CANNOT SAY

WHAT CRITERIA DO WE USE TO DECIDE IF TRADE DISTRIBUTION IS APPROPRIATE?

Firstly, we will only consider a distribution relationship with publishers who have a UK-based storage and representation arrangement. Generally, we will hold a larger stock than would normally be required of a wholesaler, but we do need to have easy access to top-up facilities within the UK.

In addition, it is imperative that the titles are represented to the trade in order to generate UK sales. Whether this is via a UK-based sales/marketing presence, or one based overseas, is not important, as long as it is effective in selling the titles to the target audience. Although we offer some promotional assistance through our weekly/monthly publications we do not offer sales and marketing as a service per se.

MINIMUM TURNOVER/LINES

The publisher should normally be able to demonstrate a realistic expectation of turnover in excess of £50k per annum at RRP and have a minimum of 5 lines. However, these targets are both negotiable where appropriate.

WHAT TERMS WILL BE REQUIRED?

Final discount and credit terms will be agreed on a case-by-case basis. Stock will be held on a consignment basis and we will provide monthly statements of sales and other management information. Invoicing will be against sales achieved each month and within the credit terms agreed.

Q7a. All invoices are paid 30 days in arrears.

A - TRUE	B - FALSE	C - CANNOT SAY

Q7b. An application from a publisher with a turnover of £49k will be accepted.

A - TRUE	B - FALSE	C - CANNOT SAY

Q7c. Applicants who reside in southern Ireland will not be considered for a trade account.

A - TRUE	B - FALSE	C - CANNOT SAY

THE ROLE OF THE AMBULANCE SERVICE

Most people believe that the Ambulance Service is simply there to respond to emergency incidents such as road traffic collisions (RTCs), seriously ill or injured patients, fires and other such incidents. While these are the core roles that the service undertakes, there are also a number of other important duties that are carried out, such as patient transport services.

The latter is carried out by the employees of the Ambulance Service, who carry disabled, elderly and vulnerable people to and from out-patient appointments, hospital admissions and also to and from day centres and clinics. Behind the operational ambulance crew is a team of people who have different roles, all designed to provide the necessary support required that is so valued by the community.

To begin with, there are the 999 call operators who take the initial calls. Their job is to gather as much information as possible about the emergency call, the nature of the incident, its location and the level of response that is required.

These people are integral to the Ambulance Service and are crucial to patient care. For example, if a patient is critically ill they may need to talk the caller through a life-saving procedure while they wait for the ambulance crews to get there.

Q8a. The 999 call operators do not travel in the ambulance with the paramedics.

A - TRUE	B - FALSE	C - CANNOT SAY

Q8b. Responding to road traffic collisions forms part of the core role of the Ambulance Service.

A - TRUE	B - FALSE	C - CANNOT SAY

Q8c. 999 call operators may need to talk the caller through a life-saving procedure while they wait for the ambulance crews to get there.

A - TRUE	B - FALSE	C - CANNOT SAY

WHAT IS A CUSTOMER CHARTER?

A Customer Charter is a statement as to how a company will deliver a quality customer service. The main purpose of a Customer Charter is to inform customers of the standards of service to expect, what to do if something goes wrong and how to make a complaint. In addition to this a Customer Charter also helps employees by setting out clearly defined standards of how they should perform within the organisation in relation to customer service delivery.

IS IT NECESSARY FOR AN ORGANISATION TO HAVE ONE?

Whilst not a legal requirement, a Customer Charter is an ideal way of helping organisations define what that service should be and the standard that should be expected. The charter will also help customers get the most from an organisation's services, including how to make a complaint if they are dissatisfied with any aspect of service or if they have ideas for improvement.

OTHER POINTS TO CONSIDER

A Customer Charter should be written in a clear and user-friendly manner. In addition to this, a Crystal Mark endorsement by the Plain English Campaign would enhance its status. If appropriate, it should be displayed in a prominent place, so all customers can see it. The Customer Charter must be available in different formats, such as large print and audio, so that customers with particular needs can access it. If an organisation is part of an industry where a regulator has been appointed, details of how to contact the regulator should be included.

Q9a. A Customer Charter is a legal requirement within an organisation.

A - TRUE	B - FALSE	C - CANNOT SAY

Q9b. A Customer Charter must be written using a Crystal Mark endorsement by the Plain English Campaign.

A - TRUE	B - FALSE	C - CANNOT SAY

Q9c. The Customer Charter may be available in different formats, such as large print and audio, so that customers with particular needs can access it.

A - TRUE	B - FALSE	C - CANNOT SAY

WHAT IS A BALANCE SHEET?

A balance sheet is a snapshot of a company's financial position at a particular point in time. In contrast, an income statement measures income over a period of time.

A balance sheet is usually calculated for March 31, last day of the financial year. A financial year starts on April 1 and ends on March 31. For example, the period between April 1, 2011 and March 31, 2012 will complete a financial year. A balance sheet measures three kinds of variables: assets, liabilities and shareholder's equity.

Assets are things like factories and machinery that the company uses to create value for its customers. Liabilities are what the company owes to third parties (eg outstanding payments to suppliers). Equity is the money initially invested by shareholders plus the retained earnings over the years. These three variables are linked by the relationship: Assets = Liabilities + Shareholder's equity. Both assets and liabilities are further classified based on their liquidity, that is, how easily they can be converted into cash.

Current liabilities are liabilities that are due within a year and include interest payments, dividend payments and accounts payable. Long-term assets include fixed assets like land and factories as well as intangible assets like goodwill and brands. Finally, long-term liabilities are basically debt with maturity of more than a year.

Q10a. A financial year starts on March 31, the last day of the financial year, and ends on April 1.

A - TRUE	B - FALSE	C - CANNOT SAY

Q10b. It can be said that the liquidity of both assets and liabilities is how easily they can be converted into cash.

A - TRUE	B - FALSE	C - CANNOT SAY

Q10c. A balance sheet is a legal requirement and every company must have one.

A - TRUE	B - FALSE	C - CANNOT SAY

Now that you have reached the end of the test, check your answers with the ones that are provided in the next section.

ANSWERS AND EXPLANATIONS TO VERBAL REASONING TEST 1

ANALYSTS PROVE FORECASTERS WRONG

The Office for National Statistics (ONS) said internet shopping and sales of household goods had been better in October compared with previous months. However, sales of clothing and footwear, where many retailers cut prices before Christmas, were particularly weak.

b: The increase came as a surprise to many analysts who were predicting a 0.4% fall in internet shopping and sales of household goods. The rise meant that retail sale volumes in the three months leading up to January were up by 2.6% on the previous quarter. The final quarter of the year is a better guide to the underlying trend than one month's figures.

Some analysts cautioned that the heavy seasonal adjustment of the raw spending figures at the turn of the year made interpreting the data difficult. Even so, the government will be relieved that spending appears to be holding up c: despite the squeeze on incomes caused by high inflation, rising unemployment, a weak housing market and the crisis in the eurozone.

Retail sales account for less than half of total consumer spending and do not include the purchase of cars or eating out. The ONS said that its measure of inflation in the high street – the annual retail sales deflator – fell to 2.2% last month, its lowest level since November 2009. a: Ministers are hoping that lower inflation will boost real income growth during the course of 2012.

Q1a. Ministers hope that higher inflation will boost real income growth during 2012.

Answer - B (FALSE)

The passage states that ministers hope that 'lower' inflation will boost real income growth, not higher. Therefore, the statement is false.

Q1b. Analysts predicted a 0.4% rise in the sales of household goods.

Answer - B (FALSE)

The passage states that analysts were predicting a 0.4% fall in sales of household goods, not rise. Therefore, the statement is false.

Q1c. The crisis in the eurozone is contributing to the squeeze on incomes.

Answer - A (TRUE)

This statement is true based on the information provided in the passage.

LONG-SERVICE PAYMENTS

[b]: <u>Employees who attain fifteen years' continuous service between 7th November 2003 and 30th June 2007 shall qualify for the long-service payment at the rate applicable at the time.</u> Employees who are promoted to a higher role during this period will cease to qualify for the payment but will receive a minimum pay increase on promotion of £300 per annum, which will be achieved through partial protection of the long-service payment.

Where the pay assimilation process on 7th November 2003 created a basic pay increase of more than 7%, and the employee was in receipt of the long-service payment, the payment has been reduced with effect from that date by the amount that the increase exceeded 7%. The consequent pay rates were set out in circular NJC/01/04.

PAY PROTECTION FOR EMPLOYEES ON THE RETAINED DUTY SYSTEM

[a]: <u>Where an employee on the retained duty system has not received a pay increase of at least 7% (for the same pattern and level of activity) following full implementation of the pay award effective from 7th November 2003, the fire and rescue authority may introduce arrangements to ensure that such an increase is achieved.</u>

ACTING UP AND TEMPORARY PROMOTION

The NJC recognises that in the early stages of implementing the Integrated Personal Development System it may, on occasions, be difficult to apply the principles at Paragraph 19 of Section 4 Part B. Fire and rescue authorities, employees and trade unions should therefore adopt a co-operative and common sense approach to any problems that might arise.

Q2a. If an employee who is on the retained duty system has not received a pay increase of at least 7% following the implementation of the pay award, the fire and rescue service must introduce arrangements to ensure that such an increase is achieved.

Answer - B (FALSE)

This statement is false because the sentence states that the fire and rescue service 'may' introduce arrangements; it does not say they 'must'.

Q2b. Employees who attain fifteen years' continuous service between 7th November 2003 and 30th June 2008 shall qualify for the long-service payment at the rate applicable at the time.

Answer - B (FALSE)

This statement is false because the sentence states 30th June 2008, instead of 30th June 2007 as stated in the passage.

Q2c. The pay assimilation process on 7th November 2003 created a basic pay increase for all employees of more than 7%.

Answer - C (CANNOT SAY)

We cannot say that this statement is true or false. It makes no reference in the passage that 'all' employees received a pay rise.

DATA WAREHOUSES

A data warehouse is the main source of information for an organisation's historical data. [c]: Its historical data is often referred to as its corporate memory. As an example of how a data warehouse can be put to good use, an organisation would use the information stored in its data warehouse to find out how many particular stock items they sold on a particular day in a particular year. [b]: They could also ascertain which employees were off sick on any given day or any given year. The data stored within the warehouse contains essential information so that managers can make appropriate management decisions.

A data warehouse is normally large in size as the information stored usually focuses on basic, structured and organised data. [a]: Some of the characteristics of the data in a data warehouse are as follows:

Time-variant - changes to the data in the database are tracked and recorded so that reports can be produced showing changes over time;

Non-volatile - the data in the database is never over-written or deleted but is retained for future reporting;

Integrated - the database contains data from most or all of an organisation's operational applications. This data is useful and meaningful for further processing and analysis.

Q3a. Integrated and non-volatile data form some of the characteristics of a data warehouse.

Answer - A (TRUE)

It is true, according to the passage, that some of the characteristics of a data warehouse include integrated and non-volatile data.

Q3b. It is not possible to identify which employees were on sick leave from the information stored in a data warehouse.

Answer - B (FALSE)

It is possible to ascertain which employees were off sick from the information stored in a data warehouse; therefore, the statement is false.

Q3c. Corporate memory is an alternative name given to historical data.

Answer - A (TRUE)

It is true that corporate memory is an alternative name given to historical data.

THE IMPORTANCE OF HEALTH AND SAFETY IN THE WORKPLACE

You must protect the safety and health of everyone in your workplace, including people with disabilities, and provide welfare facilities for your employees.

Basic things you need to consider are outlined below.

WELFARE FACILITIES

For your employees' well-being you need to provide:

- Toilets and hand basins, with soap and towels or a hand-dryer, drinking water.
- A place to store clothing (and somewhere to change if special clothing is worn for work).
- Somewhere to rest and eat meals.

HEALTH ISSUES

To have a healthy working environment, make sure there is:

- Good ventilation – a supply of fresh, clean air drawn from outside or a ventilation system.
- A reasonable working temperature (usually at least 16°C, or 13°C for strenuous work, unless other laws require lower temperatures).
- Lighting suitable for the work being carried out.
- [b]: <u>Enough room space and suitable workstations and seating.</u>
- A clean workplace with appropriate waste containers.

Q4a. It is the responsibility of the employee for keeping a workplace safe.

Answer - C (CANNOT SAY)

The passage makes no reference to this statement. Therefore, we cannot say whether the statement is true or false from the information provided. Cannot say is the correct answer.

Q4b. Providing the employee with a suitable workstation is a consideration for the employer when making the workplace safe.

Answer - A (TRUE)

We can deduce from the passage that this statement is true.

Q4c. An employer must ensure that all floor surfaces are non-slip in order to prevent slips, trips and falls.

Answer - C (CANNOT SAY)

In health and safety law this statement is true. However, the passage makes no reference it. Cannot say is the correct answer.

MAGISTRATE TRAINING

[c]: The entire selection process for becoming a magistrate can take approximately 12 months, sometimes longer depending on the area.

[a]: Once you have been accepted you will be required to undertake a comprehensive training course which is usually held over a 3-day period (18 hours). During this course you will learn the necessary skills that are required in order to become a magistrate.

The training is normally carried out by the Justice Clerk who is responsible for the court. He/she will usually be the legal advisor during your magistrate sittings. They will help you to develop all the necessary skills required in order to carry out your duties professionally and competently.

You will carry out your training as part of a group with other people who have been recruited at the same time as you. This is extremely beneficial as it will allow you to learn in a safe environment.

Training will be given using a variety of methods, which may include precourse reading, small-group work, use of case studies, computer-based training and CCTV. It is recognised that magistrates are volunteers and that their time is valuable, so every effort is made to provide all training at times and places convenient to trainees. [b]: The Ministry of Justice booklet 'Serving as a Magistrate' has more information about the magistracy and the role of magistrates.

Q5a. The comprehensive training course for becoming a magistrate usually consists of 3 days, divided into 6 hours training per day.

Answer - C (CANNOT SAY)

The passage does state that the training course is usually held over a 3-day period (18 hours). We could assume that the 18 hours are equally divided into 3 × 6 hour days. However, it is not our job to assume; we must base our answers on what is provided within the passage. Therefore, the correct answer is cannot say.

Q5b. An applicant can find out more about the role of a magistrate by reading the Ministry of Justice booklet 'Serving as a Magistrate'.

Answer - A (TRUE)

From the passage we know this statement to be true.

Q5c. The selection process for becoming a magistrate will take no longer than 12 months.

Answer - B (FALSE)

This statement is false because the passage states that the selection process can sometimes take longer than 12 months.

HOW TO ENROL IN OUR ONLINE SELLERS' PROGRAMME

To enrol in our online sellers' programme, you must have an email account, access to the Internet, have a UK distribution facility and also hold the full UK distribution rights to the item(s) you want to sell.

You must have a UK bank account capable of receiving payments via electronic bank transfer (BACS), as this is the only method of payment we offer. Each product you wish to sell in our programme must meet our minimum eligibility standards. These standards relate to quality, value, subject matter, production standards and compliance with intellectual property laws. We reserve the right to remove any products if they do not meet our standards. [b]: You are not permitted to sell any products that are deemed to be pornographic or racist.

Any books that you wish to sell via our sellers' programme must have a 10 or 13 digit ISBN number and applicable barcode printed on the back of the book in the bottom right-hand corner.

The barcode must scan to match the ISBN of the book. If the item you want to sell is a music CD then the CD must be in a protective case which meets the relevant British Standard.

The title and artist name must be printed on and readable from the spine (the thin side of the CD). [a]: Once again, the CD must contain a barcode which must scan to match the EAN or UPC.

If your item is a DVD or VHS video. Rules that apply to music CDs are also applicable to DVD products.

Q6a. The barcode on a CD must be printed on the back in the bottom right-hand corner.

Answer - C (CANNOT SAY)

The passage states that CDs require a barcode. However, no reference is made to the barcode location for CDs. Therefore the answer is cannot say.

Q6b. Pornographic products are permitted in the online sellers' programme.

Answer - B (FALSE)

The passage clearly states that pornographic products are not permitted. Therefore, the correct answer is false.

Q6c. ISBN is short for International Standard Book Number.

Answer - C (CANNOT SAY)

The passage makes no reference to this.

WHAT CRITERIA DO WE USE TO DECIDE IF TRADE DISTRIBUTION IS APPROPRIATE?

c: Firstly, we will only consider a distribution relationship with publishers who have a UK-based storage and representation arrangement. Generally we will hold a larger stock than would normally be required of a wholesaler, but we do need to have easy access to top-up facilities within the UK.

In addition, it is imperative that the titles are represented to the trade in order to generate UK sales. Whether this is via a UK-based sales/marketing presence, or one based overseas, is not important, as long as it is effective in selling the titles to the target audience. Although we offer some promotional assistance through our weekly/monthly publications we do not offer sales and marketing as a service per se.

MINIMUM TURNOVER/LINES

b: The publisher should normally be able to demonstrate a realistic expectation of turnover in excess of £50k per annum at rrp and have a minimum of 5 lines. However, these targets are both negotiable where appropriate.

WHAT TERMS WILL BE REQUIRED?

Final discount and credit terms will be agreed on a case-by-case basis. Stock will be held on a consignment basis and we will provide monthly statements of sales and other management information. a: Invoicing will be against sales achieved each month and within the credit terms agreed.

Q7a. All invoices are paid 30 days in arrears.

Answer - C (CANNOT SAY)

The passage makes no reference to this statement. The answer is cannot say from the information provided.

Q7b. An application from a publisher with a turnover of £49k will be accepted.

Answer - C (CANNOT SAY)

Although the passage makes reference to an expected turnover of £50k per annum, it also states that the targets are negotiable. Because the targets are negotiable, we cannot confirm whether the statement is true or false. As such, we must select 'cannot say' as the correct answer.

Q7c. Applicants who reside in southern Ireland will not be considered for a trade account.

Answer - C (CANNOT SAY)

The passage states that they will only consider a distribution relationship with publishers who have a UK-based storage and representation arrangement. Southern Ireland does not form part of the UK. However, the statement doesn't makes reference to applicants who 'reside' in southern Ireland. Because an applicant resides in southern Ireland we cannot say whether or not their application will be considered, simply because there is nothing to prevent a resident of southern Ireland from having a UK-based storage and representation arrangement. Therefore, the correct answer is cannot say from the information provided.

THE ROLE OF THE AMBULANCE SERVICE

Most people believe that the Ambulance Service is simply there to respond to emergency incidents such as [b]: <u>road traffic collisions (RTCs), seriously ill or injured patients, fires and other such incidents.</u> While these are the core roles that the service undertakes, there are also a number of other important duties that are carried out, such as patient transport services.

The latter is carried out by the employees of the Ambulance Service, who carry disabled, elderly and vulnerable people to and from out-patient appointments, hospital admissions and also to and from day centres and clinics. Behind the operational ambulance crew is a team of people who have different roles, all designed to provide the necessary support required that is so valued by the community.

To begin with, there are the 999 call operators who take the initial calls. Their job is to gather as much information as possible about the emergency call, the nature of the incident, its location and the level of response that is required.

These people are integral to the Ambulance Service and are crucial to patient care. For example, [c]: <u>if a patient is critically ill they may need to talk the caller through a life-saving procedure while they wait for the ambulance crews to get there.</u>

Q8a. The 999 call operators do not travel in the ambulance with the paramedics.

Answer - C (CANNOT SAY)

The passage makes no reference to this statement. The correct answer is cannot say from the information provided.

Q8b. Responding to road traffic collisions forms part of the core role of the Ambulance Service.

Answer - A (TRUE)

The passage makes it clear that responding to road traffic collisions is a core role for the Ambulance Service. The statement is true.

Q8c. 999 call operators may need to talk the caller through a life-saving procedure while they wait for the ambulance crews to get there.

Answer - A (TRUE)

From the passage we can confirm that this statement is true.

WHAT IS A CUSTOMER CHARTER?

A Customer Charter is a statement as to how a company will deliver a quality customer service. The main purpose of a Customer Charter is to inform customers of the standards of service to expect, what to do if something goes wrong and how to make a complaint. In addition to this a Customer Charter also helps employees by setting out clearly defined standards of how they should perform within the organisation in relation to customer service delivery.

IS IT NECESSARY FOR AN ORGANISATION TO HAVE ONE?

[a]: Whilst not a legal requirement, a Customer Charter is an ideal way of helping organisations define what that service should be and the standard that should be expected. The charter will also help customers get the most from an organisation's services, including how to make a complaint if they are dissatisfied with any aspect of service or if they have ideas for improvement.

OTHER POINTS TO CONSIDER

[b]: A Customer Charter should be written in a clear and user-friendly manner. In addition to this, a Crystal Mark endorsement by the Plain English Campaign would enhance its status. If appropriate, it should be displayed in a prominent place, so all customers can see it. [c]: The Customer Charter must be available in different formats, such as large print and audio, so that customers with particular needs can access it. If an organisation is part of an industry where a regulator has been appointed, details of how to contact the regulator should be included.

Q9a. A Customer Charter is a legal requirement within an organisation.

Answer - B (FALSE)

The passage clearly states that a Customer Charter is not a legal requirement. The correct answer is false.

Q9b. A Customer Charter must be written using a Crystal Mark endorsement by the Plain English Campaign.

Answer - B (FALSE)

The passage states that a Customer Charter should be written in a clear and user-friendly manner and that a Crystal Mark endorsement by the Plain English Campaign would enhance its status. However the use of a Crystal Mark is not compulsory. Therefore, the statement is false.

Q9c. The Customer Charter may be available in different formats, such as large print and audio, so that customers with particular needs can access it.

Answer - B (FALSE)

The passage states that "The Customer Charter must be available…"

The statement above states that it 'may' be available. Therefore, it is false.

WHAT IS A BALANCE SHEET?

A balance sheet is a snapshot of a company's financial position at a particular point of time in contrast to an income statement, which measures income over a period of time.

A balance sheet is usually calculated for March 31, last day of the financial year. [a]: A financial year starts on April 1 and ends on March 31. For example, the period between April 1, 2011 and March 31, 2012 will complete a financial year. A balance sheet measures three kinds of variables: assets, liabilities and shareholder's equity.

Assets are things like factories and machinery that the company uses to create value for its customers. Liabilities are what the company owes to third parties (eg outstanding payments to suppliers). Equity is the money initially invested by shareholders plus the retained earnings over the years. These three variables are linked by the relationship: Assets = Liabilities + Shareholder's equity. [b]: Both assets and liabilities are further classified based on their liquidity, that is, how easily they can be converted into cash.

Current liabilities are liabilities that are due within a year and include interest payments, dividend payments and accounts payable. Long-term assets include fixed assets like land and factories as well as intangible assets like goodwill and brands. Finally, long-term liabilities are basically debt with maturity of more than a year.

Q10a. A financial year starts on March 31 and ends on April 1.

Answer - B (FALSE)

The statement is false because the passage states that a financial year starts on April 1 and ends on March 31. The statement is therefore false.

Q10b. It can be said that the liquidity of both assets and liabilities is how easily they can be converted into cash.

Answer - A (TRUE)

The passage clearly states that both assets and liabilities are further classified based on their liquidity, that is, how easily they can be converted into cash. The correct answer is true.

Q10c. A balance sheet is a legal requirement and every company must have one.

Answer - C (CANNOT SAY)

The passage makes no reference to this statement; therefore, cannot say is the correct answer.

If you did not perform too well during the test, try not to worry. The important thing is to establish why you went wrong and to learn from the mistakes. This will enable you to gradually improve your scores.

Now move on to Verbal Reasoning Test 2. You have 10 minutes to complete the test which contains ten questions. Answers and explanations are provided at the end of the test.

VERBAL REASONING TEST 2

During Verbal Reasoning Test 2 there are 10 practice passages which each contain 3 questions. Answer each question based solely on the information provided. You must select either TRUE, FALSE or CANNOT SAY based on the information provided in the passage.

- You have 10 minutes to complete the test.

- Concentrate fully on each test.

- If unsure of an answer you should select the one that you believe to be correct.

- Avoid all forms of wild guessing.

Once you have completed the test check your answers with the ones that are provided.

how2become.com

VERBAL REASONING
TEST 2

Number of Passages = 10

Questions per Passage = 3

Total Number of Questions = 30

Surname:

Forename:

Date of Test (dd/mm/yyyy):

Allotted Time = 10 Minutes

LEARNING THE TRAIN DRIVER'S ROUTE KNOWLEDGE

Competence in the train driver's route knowledge is extremely important, simply because trains have such a long stopping distance. As an example, a train travelling at a speed of 200 km/h can take three miles to stop. If the driver lacks route knowledge, then stopping distances can be compromised. Stopping distances can be greatly affected by the weight of a train. Trains cannot be driven on line-of-sight like road vehicles because the driver has to know what is up-ahead in order to operate the train safely. This is why route knowledge is so important to the role of a train driver.

During initial training a trainee driver will be given a Route Learning Ticket. This gives the driver authority to travel in the cab whilst they learn the routes under supervision of a qualified instructor or qualified train driver. However, visual aids such as videos and visual learning platforms are being introduced so that drivers can learn the routes in a more controlled environment.

In order to successfully pass the route knowledge assessment a driver must learn all of the stations, speed restrictions, signals, signal boxes, level crossings, gradients and other features that are applicable to the role.

The assessment is either with a question and answer session in front of the manager or with a multiple choice route assessment package on a computer.

Q1a. A train's stopping distance is increased by the weight of the train.

A - TRUE	B - FALSE	C - CANNOT SAY

Q1b. A train travelling at a speed of 400 km/h will take six miles to stop.

A - TRUE	B - FALSE	C - CANNOT SAY

Q1c. Learning speed restrictions and stations will help towards passing the route knowledge assessment.

A - TRUE	B - FALSE	C - CANNOT SAY

SENDING FRANKED MAIL

You have the option of a one-off collection or a regular daily collection at a pre-arranged time. You can print and complete the form for a regular collection, or if you require a one-off collection or wish to discuss your collection requirements in more detail you can call the Business Relations Manager.

If you need to carry out an urgent same day mailing and would like your mail collected, you'll need to let us know before 12.00pm the same day by calling the Business Support telephone number. We will then arrange a single collection from your premises.

WEEKEND COLLECTIONS

We cannot collect on Saturdays or Sundays without prior arrangement. If you are interested in arranging a weekend collection for your business then please contact your allocated business support manager. A turnover in excess of £2500 per annum is required for this service. Any franked mail inaccuracies will be rejected.

PREPARING FRANKED MAIL FOR COLLECTION

1. Be sure to address your mail correctly, using the correct postcode and postage.
2. Bundle all franked mail together, with the addresses facing the same direction.
3. Bundle different types of mail separately.
4. Put stamped mail in separate bags.
5. Weigh each pouch, bag or tray, checking that they're less than 11kg (to comply with the health and safety limit).
6. Check that all your mail is ready for collection on time and at your collection point.

Q2a. Saturday collections can be arranged with prior arrangement.

A - TRUE	B - FALSE	C - CANNOT SAY

Q2b. The health and safety limit for a bag of mail is less than 11kg.

A - TRUE	B - FALSE	C - CANNOT SAY

Q2c. Bundled franked mail with the addresses that are not facing the same direction will be rejected.

A - TRUE	B - FALSE	C - CANNOT SAY

BUSINESS FRANCHISE INFORMATION

Franchises are very popular at the moment with increasing numbers of people choosing to buy one as opposed to starting out by setting up their own business. By purchasing a franchise you are effectively taking advantage of the success of an already established business. As the 'franchisee', you are buying a licence to use the name, products, services, and management support systems of the "franchiser" company. This licence normally covers a particular geographical area and runs for a limited time. The downside to a franchise is that you will never actually legally own the business.

As a franchisee, the way you pay for the franchise may be through an initial fee, ongoing management fees, a share of your turnover, or a combination of these depending on how you have set up the franchise. A franchise business can take different legal forms - most are sole traders, partnerships or limited companies. Whatever the structure, the franchisee's freedom to manage the business is limited by the terms of the franchise agreement.

There is information to suggest that the franchise business sector is still growing rapidly. During 2007 the Natwest Bank carried out a survey into the UK franchise market which revealed the astonishing financial growth of this sector. The approximate annual turnover of the business franchise sector is in excess of £10.8 billion.

What is more interesting to note is that the vast majority of business franchisees in 2007 were in profit - a total of 93% to be exact. In 1991 the total number of profitable franchisees was 70% and in 2004 it was 88%. Therefore, this business sector is growing.

Q3a. During 2007 the total number of business franchises that were not in profit totalled 7%.

A - TRUE	B - FALSE	C - CANNOT SAY

Q3b. As the 'franchiser', you are buying a licence to use the name, products, services, and management support systems of the 'franchisee' company.

A - TRUE	B - FALSE	C - CANNOT SAY

Q3c. A franchise business can take different legal forms including Limited Liability Partnership (LLP).

A - TRUE	B - FALSE	C - CANNOT SAY

COMPANY ORDERING PROCESS

1.1 Our display of products and online services on our website is an invitation and not an offer to sell those goods to you.

1.2 An offer is made when you place the order for your products or online service. However, we will not have made a contract with you unless and until we accept your offer.

1.3 We take payment from your card when we process your order and have checked your card details. Goods are subject to availability. If we are unable to supply the goods, we will inform you of this as soon as possible. A full refund will be given if you have already paid for the goods. It is our aim to always keep our website updated and all goods displayed available.

1.4 If you enter a correct email address we will send you an order acknowledgement email immediately and receipt of payment. These do not constitute an order confirmation or order acceptance from us.

1.5 Unless we have notified you that we do not accept your order or you have cancelled it, order acceptance and the creation of the contract between you and us will take place at the point the goods you have ordered are dispatched.

1.6 The contract will be formed at the place of dispatch of the goods. All goods, wherever possible, will be dispatched within 24 hours of the order being placed, Monday to Thursday. If your order falls on a weekend or bank holiday, your order will be dispatched on the next available working day. All orders that are sent via recorded delivery will require a signature. In the majority of cases, however, we will dispatch goods using Royal Mail's standard First Class delivery service.

Q4a. If a customer places an order, and they have entered a correct email address, they will immediately receive an order confirmation email.

A - TRUE	B - FALSE	C - CANNOT SAY

Q4b. Orders placed on a Friday will be dispatched on a Saturday.

A - TRUE	B - FALSE	C - CANNOT SAY

Q4c. Payment is taken from the card once the card details have been checked.

A - TRUE	B - FALSE	C - CANNOT SAY

THE HISTORY OF FOOTBALL

The earliest records of a game similar to football as we know it today are from China in 206 BC. By AD 500, round footballs stuffed with hair were in use. It is suggested that Roman legions may have introduced the game to Europe and England in particular during the Roman occupation from AD 40 to AD 400.

The game increased in popularity, developing into 'mob games' called mêlées, or mellays, in which a ball, usually an inflated animal bladder, was advanced by kicking, punching and carrying. As many as 100 players from two towns or parishes started at a mid-point and used their localities' limits as goals. King Richard II of England banned the game in 1389 because it interfered with archery practice, and later monarchs issued similar proscriptions into the 15th century, to little effect.

By the middle of the 19th century it was decided that uniformity of the rules was necessary so that every team could play the same game. Therefore the Football Association (FA) was formed in England and during the latter part of 1863, following a series of meetings, the first rules of the game of football were laid down. The first rules were based on those that had been in use at Cambridge University at the time. Some of the first rules also known as the Laws of the Game (there were 14 in total) included:

Rule 1. The maximum length of the ground shall be 200 yards; the maximum breadth shall be 100 yards; the length and breadth shall be marked off with flags; and the goals shall be defined by two upright posts, 8 yards apart, without any tape or bar across them.

Rule 10. Neither tripping nor hacking shall be allowed, and no player shall use his hands to hold or push an adversary.

Q5a. By the middle of the 19th century it was decided that uniforms would be worn by referees.

A - TRUE	B - FALSE	C - CANNOT SAY

Q5b. King Richard II of England practised archery.

A - TRUE	B - FALSE	C - CANNOT SAY

Q5c. According to the passage there were four Laws of the Game.

A - TRUE	B - FALSE	C - CANNOT SAY

RECONNAISSANCE

Reconnaissance is a crucial aspect of close protection activity, military operations, and civilian protection from man-made and natural hazards. It is used by meteorological and environmental services as well as a whole host of other agencies needing to ascertain risk of danger. These days, the term is much more commonly replaced by 'human intelligence' and practised by specialised units.

The word reconnaissance entered the English language around 1810 - not coincidentally of course during the period when the British were at war with Napoleon's French army. It derives from the French word literally meaning to 'recognise'.

Reconnaissance refers to an operation whose objectives are to obtain information by employing a number of detection techniques. The information required for a close protection operative would centre around the identification, intent and risk component of a potential 'enemy' securing evidence of their motivation methods and hence employing threat assessment and risk management strategies as part of the operational goals.

A close protection operative would, for example, use route reconnaissance, assessing a planned route of their principals' journey and identifying risk areas. A similar process would be employed in carrying out venue reconnaissance. Here a venue would be pre-checked by the close protection team, assessing the effectiveness of emergency exits and meeting points and implementing pre-planned strategies to deal with potential risk.

Q6a. A close protection team would pre-check a venue in order to assess the effectiveness of pre-planned strategies to deal with potential risk.

A - TRUE	B - FALSE	C - CANNOT SAY

Q6b. Reconnaissance is often referred to as RECON within the industry.

A - TRUE	B - FALSE	C - CANNOT SAY

Q6c. It is a coincidence that the word reconnaissance entered the English language during the period when the British were at war with France.

A - TRUE	B - FALSE	C - CANNOT SAY

EQUALITY AND FAIRNESS IN THE FIRE SERVICE

Under the Race Relations (Amendment) Act, public authorities (including the Fire and Rescue Service) have a general duty to promote race equality. The Fire Service does not accept any form of racism. This means that when carrying out their functions or duties they must have due regard for the need to:

· Eliminate unlawful discrimination.

· Promote equality of opportunity.

· Promote good relations between persons of different racial groups.

In order to demonstrate how a Fire and Rescue Service plan to meet their statutory duties, they have an obligation to produce and publish what is called a Race Equality Scheme. The Race Equality Scheme outlines their strategy and action plan to ensure that equality and diversity are mainstreamed through their policies, practices, procedures and functions. Central to this strategy are external consultation, monitoring and assessment, training, and ensuring that the public has access to this information.

"Equality is not about treating everybody the same, but recognising we are all individuals, unique in our own way. Equality and fairness is about recognising, accepting and valuing people's unique individuality accord- ing to their needs. This often means that individuals may be treated appropriately, yet fairly, based on their needs."

Q7a. Any form of racism is unacceptable in the Fire Service.

A - TRUE	B - FALSE	C - CANNOT SAY

Q7b. The general public does have access to the Race Equality Scheme.

A - TRUE	B - FALSE	C - CANNOT SAY

Q7c. The Fire Service may promote good relations between persons of different racial groups.

A - TRUE	B - FALSE	C - CANNOT SAY

CENTRAL HEATING SYSTEM

Over half the money spent on fuel bills in the UK goes towards providing heating and hot water. Therefore, having an efficient boiler and central heating system is crucial to helping you to reduce costs. If your boiler and central heating system are in a poor state of repair, this can add up to an extra third on your heating bills.

In order to save money on your heating bills you must first of all under- stand your current system. The vast majority of homes in the UK have either a central heating system, consisting of a boiler and radiators, or they use electric storage heaters. This is the most common form of heat- ing in the UK. A single boiler heats up water that is pumped through pipes to radiators throughout the house as well as providing hot water for the kitchen and bathroom taps.

Gas, oil and LPG boilers may be combination boilers, in which case they heat the hot water as it is needed and don't need to store it. Otherwise, the boiler heats up water and it is stored in a hot water cylinder that then feeds the taps. If you have a system like this, your options for energy-saving improvements include:

·   Replacing your current boiler with a more modern/efficient model.

·   Fitting better controls to your system.

·   Using the controls on your current system to only generate heat where and when you want it.

·   Switching to a cheaper or lower carbon fuel or technology such as wood-fuelled or solar water heating.

·   Making any insulation and draught-proofing improvements that you can.

Q8a. Most people in the UK are concerned about rising fuel bills.

A - TRUE	B - FALSE	C - CANNOT SAY

Q8b. If your boiler and central heating system are in a poor state of repair, this can add over an extra third on your heating bills.

A - TRUE	B - FALSE	C - CANNOT SAY

Q8c. If you have a combination boiler system, one of your options for energy-saving improvements is fitting better controls to your system.

A - TRUE	B - FALSE	C - CANNOT SAY

THE HISTORY OF THE SAS

The Special Air Service was originally founded by Lieutenant David Stirling during World War II. The initial purpose of the regiment was to be a long-range desert patrol group required to conduct raids and sabotage operations far behind enemy lines.

Lieutenant Stirling was a member of Number 8 Commando Regiment and he specifically looked for recruits who were both talented and individual specialists in their field, and who also had initiative.

The first mission of the SAS turned out to be a disaster. They were operating in support of Field Marshal Claude Auchinleck's attack in November 1941, but only 22 out of 62 SAS troopers deployed reached the rendezvous point. However, Stirling still managed to organise another attack against the German airfields at Aqedabia, Site and Agheila, which successfully destroyed 61 enemy aircraft without a single casualty. After that, the 1st SAS earned regimental status and Stirling's brother Bill began to arrange a second regiment called Number 2 SAS.

It was during the desert war that they performed a number of successful insertion missions and destroyed many aircraft and fuel depots in the process. Their success contributed towards Hitler issuing his Kommandobefehl order to execute all captured Commandos. The Germans then stepped up security and as a result the SAS changed their tactics. They used jeeps armed with Vickers K machine guns and used tracer ammunition to ignite fuel and aircraft. When the Italians captured David Stirling, he ended up in Colditz Castle as a prisoner of war for the remainder of the war. His brother, Bill Stirling, and 'Paddy' Blair Mayne, then took command of the regiment.

Q9a. During the SAS's first mission only 42 of the total troopers deployed reached the rendezvous point.

A - TRUE	B - FALSE	C - CANNOT SAY

Q9b. When the Germans captured David Stirling, he ended up in Colditz Castle as a prisoner of war for the remainder of the conflict.

A - TRUE	B - FALSE	C - CANNOT SAY

Q9c. Lieutenant Stirling was a member of Number 8 SAS Regiment.

A - TRUE	B - FALSE	C - CANNOT SAY

HOW TO MEND A BICYCLE PUNCTURE

1. In order to mend a bicycle puncture you will first of all require a puncture repair kit, a pump, tyre levers, sandpaper, marking chalk and glue.

2. The first step is to stand the bike upside down on its saddle. Take off the effected wheel using the quick-release lever on the hub or, if the wheel is bolted on, undo with a spanner.

3. Take one of the tyre levers and slide the flat end between the rim and the tyre. Then, bend back the tyre lever and hook it on to one of the spokes. Take the next lever and do the same about 5 cm further around the tyre. Remove the first lever then move it further along the rim and use it to pry off the tyre again until one side is free.

4. Take the inner tube out and inflate. Check for thorns, wire or anything that may have caused the puncture. Take the tyre fully off the rim and inspect inside and outside for glass or debris. Check the rim to make sure no spoke ends have worn through the rim strip.

5. Hold the inflated tube to your ear: you may be able to hear air escaping. If you can't find the spot, hold part of the tube under water and watch for bubbles. Slowly move the tube through the water. Once you find the puncture, mark it with chalk or a crayon.

6. Dry the inner tube. Rough the area around the hole with sandpaper. Cover an area the size of a 20p coin around the puncture with glue. Leave until it gets tacky.

7. Place a patch centred over the puncture. Smooth out and make sure there are no air bubbles. Leave to dry for about 10 minutes.

8. Put one side of the tyre back on the rim. Place the tube back inside the tyre, beginning at the valve and working around the tyre. It should be slightly inflated.

9. Now, using the tyre levers, begin putting the free side of the tyre back inside the rim. Start near the valve and work the levers around in opposite directions. Be careful not to pinch the inner tube.

10. When you are left with about 15 cm still loose, it might be difficult to get the tyre back on. Use two tyre levers to keep each end of the loose bit of tyre in place, and then use the third to pop the tyre wall back inside the rim.

Q10a. A cause of punctures might be that spoke ends have worn through the rim strip.

A - TRUE	B - FALSE	C - CANNOT SAY

Q10b. When putting the repaired wheel back onto the bicycle you will need to tighten the quick-release levers or redo the bolts with a spanner.

A - TRUE	B - FALSE	C - CANNOT SAY

Q10c. When you place the tube back inside the tyre it should be slightly deflated.

A - TRUE	B - FALSE	C - CANNOT SAY

Now check your answers with the ones that follow. We have provided full explanations to the answers in order to assist you.

ANSWERS AND EXPLANATIONS TO VERBAL REASONING TEST 2

LEARNING THE TRAIN DRIVER'S ROUTE KNOWLEDGE

Competence in the train driver's route knowledge is extremely important, simply because trains have such a long stopping distance. [b]: <u>As an example, a train travelling at a speed of 200 km/h can take three miles to stop.</u> If the driver lacks route knowledge, then stopping distances can be compromised. [a]: <u>Stopping distances can be greatly affected by the weight of a train.</u> Trains cannot be driven on line- of-sight like road vehicles because the driver has to know what is up ahead in order to operate the train safely. This is why route knowledge is so important to the role of a train driver.

During initial training a trainee driver will be given a Route Learning Ticket. This gives the driver authority to travel in the cab whilst they learn the routes under supervision with a qualified instructor or qualified train driver. However, visual aids such as videos and visual learning platforms are being introduced so that drivers can learn the routes in a more controlled environment.

[c]: <u>In order to successfully pass the route knowledge assessment a driver must learn all of the stations, speed restrictions, signals, signal boxes, level crossings, gradients and other features that are applicable to the role.</u>

The assessment is either with a question and answer session in front of the manager or with a multiple choice route assessment package on a computer.

Q1a. A train's stopping distance is increased by the weight of the train.

Answer - C (CANNOT SAY)

Whilst common sense would dictate that a train's stopping distance will increase by its weight we can only answer the question based on information provided. The passage states that stopping distances can be greatly affected by weight; however, it does not confirm that the stopping distance is increased by the weight. Therefore, we must choose cannot say.

Q1b. A train travelling at a speed of 400 km/h will take six miles to stop.

Answer - C (CANNOT SAY)

The passage states that a train travelling at a speed of 200km/h can take three miles to stop. You could be forgiven for assuming that a train travelling at 400 km/h would take six miles to stop. However, the passage does not confirm this and therefore we must select cannot say as the correct answer.

Q1c. Learning speed restrictions and stations will help towards passing the route knowledge assessment.

Answer - A (TRUE)

This is made clear by the third paragraph.

SENDING FRANKED MAIL

You have the option of a one-off collection or a regular daily collection at a pre-arranged time. You can print and complete the form for a regular collection, or if you require a one-off collection or wish to discuss your collection requirements in more detail you can call the Business Relations Manager.

If you need to carry out an urgent same day mailing and would like your mail collected, you'll need to let us know before 12.00pm the same day by calling the Business Support telephone number. We will then arrange a single collection from your premises.

WEEKEND COLLECTIONS

[a]: We cannot collect on Saturdays or Sundays without prior arrangement. If you are interested in arranging a weekend collection for your business then please contact your allocated business support manager. A turnover in excess of £2500 per annum is required for this service. Any franked mail inaccuracies will be rejected.

PREPARING FRANKED MAIL FOR COLLECTION

1. Be sure to address your mail correctly, using the correct postcode and postage.

2. [c]: Bundle all franked mail together, with the addresses facing the same direction.

3. Bundle different types of mail separately.

4. Put stamped mail in separate bags.

5. [b]: Weigh each pouch, bag or tray, checking that they're less than 11kg (to comply with the health and safety limit).

6. Check that all your mail is ready for collection on time and at your collection point.

Q2a. Saturday collections can be arranged with prior arrangement.

Answer - A (TRUE)

The passage states that they cannot collect on Saturdays or Sundays without prior arrangement. Therefore, the statement is true.

Q2b. The health and safety limit for a bag of mail is less than 11kg.

Answer - A (TRUE)

The passage indicates that less than 11kg is the health and safety limit; therefore, the correct answer is true.

Q2c. Bundled franked mail with the addresses that are not facing the same direction will be rejected.

Answer - A (TRUE)

In paragraph 3 of the passage it states that any franked mail inaccuracies will be rejected. The statement is true.

BUSINESS FRANCHISE INFORMATION

Franchises are very popular at the moment with increasing numbers of people choosing to buy one as opposed to starting out by setting up their own business. By purchasing a franchise you are effectively taking advantage of the success of an already established business. [b]: <u>As the 'franchisee', you are buying a licence to use the name, products, services, and management support systems of the 'franchiser' company.</u> This licence normally covers a particular geographical area and runs for a limited time. The downside to a franchise is that you will never actually legally own the business.

As a franchisee, the way you pay for the franchise may be through an initial fee, ongoing management fees, a share of your turnover, or a combination of these depending on how you have set up the franchise. [c]: <u>A franchise business can take different legal forms - most are sole traders, partnerships or limited companies.</u> Whatever the structure, the franchisee's freedom to manage the business is limited by the terms of the franchise agreement.

There is information to suggest that the franchise business sector is still growing rapidly. During 2007 the Natwest Bank carried out a survey into the UK franchise market which revealed the astonishing financial growth of this sector. The approximate annual turnover of the business franchise sector is in excess of £10.8 billion. [a]: <u>What is more interesting to note is that the vast majority of business franchisees in 2007 were in profit - a total of 93% to be exact.</u> In 1991 the total number of profitable franchisees was 70% and in 2004 it was 88%. Therefore, this business sector is growing.

Q3a. During 2007 the total number of business franchises that were not in profit totalled 7%.

Answer - A (TRUE)

The passage states that 93% of business franchises in 2007 were in profit. This means that 7% were not in profit. The correct answer is true.

Q3b. As the 'franchiser', you are buying a licence to use the name, products, services, and management support systems of the 'franchisee' company.

Answer - B (FALSE)

The passage states "As the 'franchisee', you are buying a licence to use the name, products, services, and management support systems of the 'franchiser' company". The correct answer is false.

Q3c. A franchise business can take different legal forms including Limited Liability Partnership (LLP).

Answer - C (CANNOT SAY)

We cannot state whether this sentence is true or false from the information provided. The passage states only that "a franchise business can take different legal forms". We cannot assume that this includes Limited Liability Partnerships (LLP). The correct answer is cannot say.

COMPANY ORDERING PROCESS

1.1 Our display of products and online services on our website is an invitation and not an offer to sell those goods to you.

1.2 An offer is made when you place the order for your products or online service. However, we will not have made a contract with you unless and until we accept your offer.

1.3 ^c: <u>We take payment from your card when we process your order and have checked your card details.</u> Goods are subject to availability. If we are unable to supply the goods, we will inform you of this as soon as possible. A full refund will be given if you have already paid for the goods. It is our aim to always keep our website updated and all goods displayed available.

1.4 ^a: <u>If you enter a correct email address we will send you an order acknowl-edgement email immediately and receipt of payment.</u> These do not constitute an order confirmation or order acceptance from us.

1.5 Unless we have notified you that we do not accept your order or you have cancelled it, order acceptance and the creation of the contract between you and us will take place at the point the goods you have ordered are dispatched.

1.6 ^b: <u>The contract will be formed at the place of dispatch of the goods. All goods, wherever possible, will be dispatched within 24 hours of the order being placed, Monday to Thursday.</u> If your order falls on a weekend or bank holiday, your order will be dispatched on the next available working day. All orders that are sent via recorded delivery will require a signature. In the majority of cases, however, we will dispatch goods using Royal Mail's standard First Class delivery service.

Q4a. If a customer places an order, and they have entered a correct email address, they will immediately receive an order confirmation email.

Answer - B (FALSE)

The passage states that if a correct email address is entered they will send the customer an order acknowledgment email. It goes on to state that this email is not an order confirmation. The correct answer is false.

Q4b. Orders placed on a Friday will be dispatched on a Saturday.

Answer - C (CANNOT SAY)

The passage states "If your order falls on a weekend or bank holiday, your order will be dispatched on the next available working day". Although we could assume that the next 'working day' is Monday, this cannot be confirmed by the text in the passage. It could quite possibly be that the company classes Saturday as a working day. Therefore, the correct answer is cannot say based on the information provided.

Q4c. Payment is taken from the card once the card details have been checked.

Answer - A (TRUE)

From the information provided in the passage we can confirm that this sentence is true.

THE HISTORY OF FOOTBALL

The earliest records of a game similar to football as we know it today are from China in 206 BC. By AD 500, round footballs stuffed with hair were in use. It is suggested that Roman legions may have introduced the game to Europe and England in particular during the Roman occupation from AD 40 to AD 400.

The game increased in popularity, developing into 'mob games' called mêlées, or mellays, in which a ball, usually an inflated animal bladder, was advanced by kicking, punching and carrying. As many as 100 players from two towns or parishes started at a mid-point and used their localities' limits as goals. [b]: King Richard II of England banned the game in 1389 because it interfered with archery practice, and later monarchs issued similar proscriptions into the 15th century, to little effect.

[a]: By the middle of the 19th century it was decided that uniformity of the rules was necessary so that every team could play the same game. Therefore the Football Association (FA) was formed in England and dur- ing the latter part of 1863, following a series of meetings, the first rules of the game of football were laid down. The first rules were based on those that had been in use at Cambridge University at the time. [c]: Some of the first rules also known as the Laws of the Game (there were 14 in total) included:

Rule 1. The maximum length of the ground shall be 200 yards; the maximum breadth shall be 100 yards; the length and breadth shall be marked off with flags; and the goals shall be defined by two upright posts, 8 yards apart, without any tape or bar across them.

Rule 10. Neither tripping nor hacking shall be allowed, and no player shall use his hands to hold or push an adversary.

Q5a. By the middle of the 19th century it was decided that uniforms would be worn by referees.

Answer - C (CANNOT SAY)

Although the passage makes reference to the 19th century and unifor- mity, it does not make reference to referees wearing uniforms. The correct answer is cannot say from the information provided.

Q5b. King Richard II of England practised archery.

Answer - C (CANNOT SAY)

This is a tricky one that may catch some people out! The passage states that King Richard II of England banned the game in 1389 because it interfered with archery practice. However, the passage does not state that it was he who practised archery. Therefore, the correct answer is cannot say.

Q5c. According to the passage there were four Laws of the Game.

Answer - B (FALSE)

The sentence is false. The passage states that there were fourteen Laws of the Game.

RECONNAISSANCE

Reconnaissance is a crucial aspect of close protection activity, military operations, and civilian protection from man-made and natural hazards. It is used by meteorological and environmental services as well as a whole host of other agencies needing to ascertain risk of danger. These days the term is much more commonly replaced by 'human intelligence' and practised by specialised units.

[c]: The word reconnaissance entered the English language around 1810 - not coincidentally of course during the period when the British were at war with Napoleon's French army. It derives from the French word literally meaning to 'recognise'.

Reconnaissance refers to an operation whose objectives are to obtain information by employing a number of detection techniques. The infor- mation required for a close protection operative would centre around the identification, intent and risk component of a potential 'enemy' securing evidence of their motivation methods and hence employing threat assess- ment and risk management strategies as part of the operational goals.

A close protection operative would, for example, use route reconnaissance, assessing a planned route of their principals' journey and identifying risk areas. A similar process would be employed in carrying out venue reconnaissance. [a]: Here a venue would be pre-checked by the close protection team, assessing the effectiveness of emergency exits and meeting points and implementing pre-planned strategies to deal with potential risk.

Q6a. A close protection team would pre-check a venue in order to assess the effectiveness of pre-planned strategies to deal with potential risk.

Answer - A (TRUE)

From the information provided in the passage we can confirm that this statement is true.

Q6b. Reconnaissance is often referred to as RECON within the industry.

Answer - C (CANNOT SAY)

Although the phrase RECON is commonly used within the industry we

are unable to confirm this as fact from the passage. The correct answer is cannot say.

Q6c. It is a coincidence that the word reconnaissance entered the English language during the period when the British were at war with France.

Answer - B (FALSE)

The passage states that it is not a coincidence the word entered the English language during the period when the British were at war with Napoleon's French army. Therefore, the correct answer is false.

EQUALITY AND FAIRNESS IN THE FIRE SERVICE

Under the Race Relations (Amendment) Act, public authorities (including the Fire and Rescue Service) have a general duty to promote race equality. [a]: The Fire service does not accept any form of racism. [c]: This means that when carrying out their functions or duties they must have due regard to the need to:

- Eliminate unlawful discrimination.

- Promote equality of opportunity.

- Promote good relations between persons of different racial groups.

In order to demonstrate how a Fire and Rescue Service plan to meet their statutory duties, they have an obligation to produce and publish what is called a Race Equality Scheme. The Race Equality Scheme outlines their strategy and action plan to ensure that equality and diversity are mainstreamed through their policies, practices, procedures and functions. [b]: Central to this strategy are external consultation, monitoring and assessment, training, and ensuring that the public has access to this information.

"Equality is not about treating everybody the same, but recognising we are all individuals, unique in our own way. Equality and fairness is about recognising, accepting and valuing people's unique individuality according to their needs. This often means that individuals may be treated appropriately, yet fairly, based on their needs."

Q7a. Any form of racism is unacceptable in the Fire Service.

Answer - A (TRUE)

This statement is certainly true, and is made clear in the first paragraph.

Q7b. The general public does have access to the Race Equality Scheme.

Answer - A (TRUE)

The passage states that central to the strategy is ensuring that the public has access to this information. The statement is true.

Q7c. The Fire Service may promote good relations between persons of different racial groups.

Answer - B (FALSE)

The statement states that the Fire Service may promote good relations between persons of different racial groups, whereas the passage states they must promote good relations. The correct answer is false.

CENTRAL HEATING SYSTEM

Over half the money spent on fuel bills in the UK goes towards providing heating and hot water. Therefore, having an efficient boiler and central heating system is crucial to helping you to reduce costs. [b]: <u>If your boiler and central heating system are in a poor state of repair, this can add up to an extra third on your heating bills.</u>

In order to save money on your heating bills you must first of all understand your current system. The vast majority of homes in the UK have either a central heating system, consisting of a boiler and radiators, or they use electric storage heaters. This is the most common form of heating in the UK. A single boiler heats up water that is pumped through pipes to radiators throughout the house as well as providing hot water for the kitchen and bathroom taps.

Most boilers run on mains gas but, in areas where mains gas is not available, the boiler can run on oil, LPG (tank gas), coal or wood. Mains gas is usually the cheapest of these fuels, and it also has the lowest carbon dioxide emissions apart from wood.

[c]: <u>Gas, oil and LPG boilers may be combination boilers, in which case they heat the hot water as it is needed and don't need to store it.</u> Otherwise, the boiler heats up water and it is stored in a hot water cylinder that then feeds the taps. If you have a system like this, your options for energy-saving improvements include:

- Replacing your current boiler with a more modern/efficient model.

- Fitting better controls to your system.

- Using the controls on your current system to only generate heat where and when you want it.

- Switching to a cheaper or lower carbon fuel or technology such as wood-fuelled or solar water heating.

- Making any insulation and draught-proofing improvements that you can.

Q8a. Most people in the UK are concerned about rising fuel bills.

Answer - C (CANNOT SAY)

The passage does make reference to heating bills but not in respect of the statement. The answer is cannot say based on the information provided.

Q8b. If your boiler and central heating system are in a poor state of repair, this can add over an extra third on your heating bills.

Answer - B (FALSE)

The passage states "If your boiler and central heating system are in a poor state of repair, this can add up to an extra third on your heating bills." Because the statement refers to it adding over an extra third on your heating bills the correct answer is false.

Q8c. If you have a combination boiler system, one of your options for energy-saving improvements is fitting better controls to your system.

Answer - C (CANNOT SAY)

In respect of energy saving improvements and fitting netter controls to your system, the passage is referring to systems where the water is stored in a hot water cylinder. We cannot tell from the information in the passage if the same applies to combination boiler systems. Therefore, the correct answer is cannot say.

THE HISTORY OF THE SAS

The Special Air Service was originally founded by Lieutenant David Stirling during World War II. The initial purpose of the regiment was to be a long-range desert patrol group required to conduct raids and sabotage operations far behind enemy lines.

[c]: Lieutenant Stirling was a member of Number 8 Commando Regiment and he specifically looked for recruits who were both talented and individual specialists in their field, and who also had initiative.

[a]: The first mission of the SAS turned out to be a disaster. They were operating in support of Field Marshal Claude Auchinleck's attack in November 1941, but only 22 out of 62 SAS troopers deployed reached the rendezvous point. However, Stirling still managed to organise another attack against the German airfields at Aqedabia, Site and Agheila, which successfully destroyed 61 enemy aircraft without a single casualty. After that, the 1st SAS earned regimental status and Stirling's brother Bill began to arrange a second regiment called Number 2 SAS.

It was during the desert war that they performed a number of successful insertion missions and destroyed many aircraft and fuel depots in the process. Their success contributed towards Hitler issuing his Kommandobefehl order to execute all captured Commandos. The Germans then stepped up security and as a result the SAS changed their tactics. They used jeeps armed with Vickers K machine guns and used tracer ammunition to ignite fuel and aircraft. [b]: When the Italians captured David Stirling, he ended up in Colditz Castle as a prisoner of war for the remainder of the war. His brother, Bill Stirling, and 'Paddy' Blair Mayne, then took command of the regiment.

Q9a. During the SAS's first mission only 42 of the total troopers deployed reached the rendezvous point.
Answer - B (FALSE)
According to the passage only 22 out of 62 troopers deployed reached the rendezvous point. The answer is false.

Q9b. When the Germans captured David Stirling, he ended up in Colditz Castle as a prisoner of war for the remainder of the conflict.
Answer - B (FALSE)
The passage states that the Italians captured David Stirling, not the Germans. The correct answer is false.

Q9c. Lieutenant Stirling was a member of Number 8 SAS Regiment.
Answer - B (FALSE)
Lieutenant Stirling was a member of Number 8 Commando Regiment, not Number 8 SAS Regiment. The correct answer is false.

HOW TO MEND A BICYCLE PUNCTURE

1. In order to mend a bicycle puncture you will first of all require a puncture repair kit, a pump, tyre levers, sandpaper, marking chalk and glue.

2. The first step is to stand the bike upside down on its saddle. [b]: Take off the effected wheel using the quick-release lever on the hub or, if the wheel is bolted on, undo with a spanner.

3. Take one of the tyre levers and slide the flat end between the rim and the tyre. Then, bend back the tyre lever and hook it on to one of the spokes. Take the next lever and do the same about 5 cm further around the tyre. Remove the first lever then move it further along the rim and use it to pry off the tyre again until one side is free.

4. Take the inner tube out and inflate. Check for thorns, wire or anything that may have caused the puncture. Take the tyre fully off the rim and inspect inside and outside for glass or debris. [a]: Check the rim to make sure no spoke ends have worn through the rim strip.

5. Hold the inflated tube to your ear: you may be able to hear air escaping. If you can't find the spot, hold part of the tube under water and watch for bubbles. Slowly move the tube through the water. Once you find the puncture, mark it with chalk or a crayon.

6. Dry the inner tube. Rough the area around the hole with sandpaper. Cover an area the size of a 20p coin around the puncture with glue. Leave until it gets tacky.

7. Place a patch centred over the puncture. Smooth out and make sure there are no air bubbles. Leave to dry for about 10 minutes.

8. [c]: Put one side of the tyre back on the rim. Place the tube back inside the tyre, beginning at the valve and working around the tyre. It should be slightly inflated.

9. Now, using the tyre levers, begin putting the free side of the tyre back inside the rim. Start near the valve and work the levers around in opposite directions. Be careful not to pinch the inner tube.

10. When you are left with about 15 cm still loose, it might be difficult to get the tyre back on. Use two tyre levers to keep each end of the loose bit of tyre in place, and then use the third to pop the tyre wall back inside the rim.

Q10a. A cause of punctures might be that spoke ends have worn through the rim strip.

Answer - C (CANNOT SAY)

The passage states that you should "Check the rim to make sure no spoke ends have worn through the rim strip". The passage makes no clear link between this and punctures.

Q10b. When putting the repaired wheel back onto the bicycle you will need to tighten the quick-release levers or redo the bolts with a spanner.

Answer - C (CANNOT SAY)

The passage only makes reference to taking off the wheel, not replacing it. Therefore, the correct answer is cannot say based on the information provided in the passage.

Q10c. When you place the tube back inside the tyre it should be slightly deflated.

Answer - B (FALSE)

The passage states that it should be slightly inflated not deflated. The correct answer is false.

VERBAL REASONING TEST 3

During Verbal Reasoning Test 3 there are 5 practice passages which each contain 5 questions. Answer each question based solely on the information provided. You must select either TRUE, FALSE or CANNOT SAY based on the information provided in the passage.

- You have 10 minutes to complete the test.

- Concentrate fully on each test.

- If unsure of an answer you should select the one that you believe to be correct.

- Avoid all forms of wild guessing.

Once you have completed the test check your answers with the ones that are provided.

how2become
.com

VERBAL REASONING
TEST 3

Number of Passages = 5

Questions per Passage = 5

Total Number of Questions = 25

Surname:

Forename:

Date of Test (dd/mm/yyyy):

Allotted Time = 10 Minutes

DETAILS OF THE MEDICAL

Applicants who successfully complete the online assessment, the physical aptitude test and the interview will be invited to attend a medical assessment. Applicants must satisfy all medical requirements in order to progress to the next stage. Details of the medical are as follows:

HEALTH QUESTIONNAIRE

Applicants will be required to accurately answer questions regarding their medical history.

PHYSICAL EXAMINATION

Applicants will be required to successfully pass a medical examination by the Medical Officer. This includes, amongst others, the following five elements:

- Lung function test.
- Hearing test.
- Vision test (including colour vision).
- Urine test.
- Pathology test.

TIME

The entire employment medical assessment will take approximately 1½ hours to complete.

SUPPORTING MEDICAL INFORMATION

Applicants with pre-existing medical conditions are encouraged to bring medical reports, x-rays or other medical information to assist the Medical Officer in assessing their individual case.

CONFIDENTIALITY

All medical information collected as part of the medical assessment will be considered confidential, and will be released only with the specific written consent of the applicant, or in accordance with legal requirements.

Once the applicant has successfully passed the medical they will be invited to the next stage of the selection process.

Q1a. There are 5 different elements to the medical.

A - TRUE	B - FALSE	C - CANNOT SAY

Q1b. The physical examination will take 1½ hours to complete.

A - TRUE	B - FALSE	C - CANNOT SAY

Q1c. Applicants with pre-existing medical conditions must bring x-rays and medical reports to assist the Medical Officer.

A - TRUE	B - FALSE	C - CANNOT SAY

Q1d. The next stage of the selection process, upon successful completion of the medical, is the interview.

A - TRUE	B - FALSE	C - CANNOT SAY

Q1e. The release of confidential information collected by the Medical Officer during the medical is illegal.

A - TRUE	B - FALSE	C - CANNOT SAY

AUSTRALIAN BUSHFIRES

The summers in Australia can bring total devastation through the many bushfires which occur. Bushfires destroy livelihoods, property, machinery, eucalyptus forests and they can even spread to the suburban areas of major cities.

Although all bushfires can have a devastating effect, few of them fall under the 'disaster' category. Some of these were in:

- Victoria (2009): 173 lives were lost in this bushfire, so it is more commonly referred to as Black Saturday.
- South Australia and Victoria (1983): This claimed 76 lives and was named Ash Wednesday.
- Southern Victoria (1969): 23 lives were claimed.
- New South Wales (1968): There were 14 fatalities in this bushfire in the Blue Mountains and coastal region.
- Hobart and Southern Tasmania (1967): 62 people were killed.
- Victoria (1939): This was named Black Friday after 71 people lost their lives.

There are two different types of bushfires in Australia - grass fires and forest fires. Grass fires more commonly occur on grazing and farm land. These often destroy fences, livestock, machinery, and they sometimes claim lives. Forest fires are largely made up of eucalyptus trees. These are extremely difficult to control due to the high amounts of flammable vapour from the leaves. The bushfires are fought by large numbers of trained volunteer fire-fighters. Helicopters and light aircraft are sometimes used to make observations about the fire and some also have the capacity to carry water. Aircraft used to carry water in order to extinguish forest fires often find that the visibility is extremely poor. This prevents them from getting close enough to the fire in order to extinguish it with their quantities of water.

Aircraft are used to make observations about the fire. This includes:

- Establishing which direction the fire is travelling;
- Locating suitable grid references to make fire-breaks to prevent firespread;
- Locating nearby homes, businesses, other buildings and livestock that are in danger from the fire spreading.

Q2a. Bushfires are extinguished by large numbers of full-time trained fire-fighters.

A - TRUE	B - FALSE	C - CANNOT SAY

Q2b. In total there have been 419 fatalities from Australian bushfires since 1939.

A - TRUE	B - FALSE	C - CANNOT SAY

Q2c. Hundreds of animals are killed by the bushfires each year.

A - TRUE	B - FALSE	C - CANNOT SAY

Q2d. Aircraft deployed to extinguish bushfires struggle to get close to the fire due to the poor visibility.

A - TRUE	B - FALSE	C - CANNOT SAY

Q2e. One way to prevent a bushfire from spreading is to create a fire-break.

A - TRUE	B - FALSE	C - CANNOT SAY

AVIEMORE RAIL INCIDENT

The time is 6:37pm on Sunday the 7th of February 2010. A two-car diesel multiple unit, which has been travelling on the west Highland Line in Scotland heading towards Aviemore, has derailed and caught fire as a result. One carriage has been left in a precarious position on the 40-foot high embankment whilst the remaining three carriages have come to rest blocking both the upside and downside tracks. In addition to blocking the lines, the incident has also caused the closure of the A35 road which is located directly below the rail line.

The train involved in the incident is a First ScotRail Class 120 Turbostar unit 156TGE. The driver of the train is a 52-year-old male named as George McDermott and the train's headcode is 6Y56. Witnesses claim that the train derailed after hitting a large boulder which had come to rest on the track following a landslide. In total, there are 34 passengers on the four carriage train. There are a number of casualties. Amongst others, an elderly female who is 72-year-old is suffering from a suspected broken collar-bone; a 32-year-old male is suffering from a serious head injury and a 21-year-old pregnant female is suffering from shock and a broken finger. The Rail Control Centre has informed all oncoming trains of the incident and has operated red stop signals along the route.

The weather is severely hampering rescue operations and the Fire and Rescue Commander has indicated that there could be a significant delay before all casualties are safely removed from the scene. The local weather centre has forecast gales of up to 60 miles per hour over the next 12 hours with temperatures dropping to minus 3 degrees.

Q3a. The current temperature is minus 3 degrees.

A - TRUE	B - FALSE	C - CANNOT SAY

Q3b. The train involved in the incident is a First ScotRail Class 120 Turbostar unit 6Y56.

A - TRUE	B - FALSE	C - CANNOT SAY

Q3c. A train derailment is when the train inadvertently leaves the track.

A - TRUE	B - FALSE	C - CANNOT SAY

Q3d. In total there are three passengers injured.

A - TRUE	B - FALSE	C - CANNOT SAY

Q3e. The A35 has been affected by the incident.

A - TRUE	B - FALSE	C - CANNOT SAY

THE DEFINITION AND PURPOSE OF THE JOB

A Trainee Probation Officer is an employee of the Probation Area, appointed on a time-limited (normally two-year) contract, who is working to obtain a Diploma in Probation Studies (DipPS). Upon successful completion of training and the award of the DipPS, a Trainee Probation Officer will be eligible for appointment as a Probation Officer.

THE MAIN DUTIES AND RESPONSIBILITIES

As a person in training, the Trainee Probation Officer's principal objective is to undertake the academic work and gain the experience in probation practice necessary to acquire, practise and demonstrate the knowledge, skills, values and competencies required to obtain both the degree and the NVQ, which together constitute the DipPS. The Trainee Probation Officer's learning needs will determine the amount and nature of the work undertaken.

In the course of their training, Trainee Probation Officers will undertake work on behalf of the employing Probation Area and will provide a service to courts, penal institutions, individual Probation Area users (or persons for whom the Probation Area has a responsibility) and local communities. A Trainee Probation Officer will, therefore, be required at all times to work in accordance with the Probation Rules, National Standards, the Probation Board's policies and all other relevant enactments and policies. In particular, in all their work, Trainee Probation Officers will ensure that service delivery reflects the Probation Area's Equality of Opportunities and Anti-Discriminatory policies and will promote, especially by contributing to risk assessment and management, the Area's overriding responsibility to ensure the safety of service users, staff and the public.

Specifically, a Trainee Probation Officer will:

·   Attend all required academic teaching events, as arranged by the University, the Consortium or the Probation Area.

·   Complete the required academic assignments.

·   Observe and participate in training and other learning experiences as arranged by the Consortium or the Probation Area.

·   Undertake such work on the Probation Area's behalf as may be required.

Q4a. NVQ stands for 'National Vocational Qualification'.

A - TRUE	B - FALSE	C - CANNOT SAY

Q4b. Trainee Probation Officers will carry out work on behalf of the employing Probation Area during their training.

A - TRUE	B - FALSE	C - CANNOT SAY

Q4c. During training a Trainee Probation Officer may miss some academic teaching events.

A - TRUE	B - FALSE	C - CANNOT SAY

Q4d. The main goal of the Trainee Probation Officer is to carry out the necessary work and gain sufficient experience in order to obtain the degree and NVQ that forms part of the DipPS.

A - TRUE	B - FALSE	C - CANNOT SAY

Q4e. Trainee Probation Officers must ensure that the service they deliver is representative of the Probation Area's equality policy.

A - TRUE	B - FALSE	C - CANNOT SAY

ACCOUNT BILLING INFORMATION

There are two separate options offered for account billing:

Monthly* - This option operates on a 4-week cycle beginning on the day of account activation.

Annual - This option operates on a 365-day cycle beginning on the day of account activation.

Note: *Customers on a monthly billing cycle are billed every 4 weeks.

When your account reaches its appropriate billing day (your account's expiration date) your credit card will be automatically billed for the next billing cycle and your account expiration date will be extended by an additional 4 weeks (or 365 for annual packages) and you will receive a receipt via email. If the transaction is unsuccessful for any reason, we will attempt to re-bill your credit card for 2 consecutive days and send an unsuccessful renewal email for each unsuccessful attempt (to your accounts specified Billing Profile email address).

After your first unsuccessful renewal attempt your account status will be updated to Billing Hold Level 1. This status indicates that your account is overdue but otherwise has no direct effect on your service which will continue for up to 4 weeks following your actual expiration date.

4 WEEKS PAST ACCOUNT EXPIRATION

4 weeks after your account expires we will attempt to re-bill your credit card for two monthly payments. If successful your account expiration date will be extended by an additional 4 weeks (from bill date) and you will receive a receipt via email.

If unsuccessful your account status will be updated to Billing Hold Level 2. This status indicates that your account is now more than 4 weeks overdue and we will close all account service until payment has been received. We will attempt to re-bill your credit card for 2 consecutive days and send an unsuccessful renewal email for each unsuccessful attempt.

When your account is in this status you will still be able to log in and access both the Earn Cash page (to manage affiliate referrals) and the Renew Account page.

Q5a. The account's expiration date can be determined as the billing day.

A - TRUE	B - FALSE	C - CANNOT SAY

Q5b. Billing Hold Level 2 occurs when an attempt to take two monthly payments after an account is 4 weeks past account expiration fails.

A - TRUE	B - FALSE	C - CANNOT SAY

Q5c. Customers who opt for the monthly billing option will be billed every 4 weeks on the first day of each month.

A - TRUE	B - FALSE	C - CANNOT SAY

Q5d. For the annual billing option the first expiration date will be 365 days after account activation.

A - TRUE	B - FALSE	C - CANNOT SAY

Q5e. Billing Hold Level 1 occurs after the first successful renewal attempt.

A - TRUE	B - FALSE	C - CANNOT SAY

Now that you have completed the test check your answers with the ones that follow in the next section.

ANSWERS AND EXPLANATIONS TO VERBAL REASONING TEST 3

DETAILS OF THE MEDICAL

[d]: Applicants who successfully complete the online assessment, the physical aptitude test and the interview will be invited to attend a medical assessment. Applicants must satisfy all medical requirements in order to progress to the next stage. Details of the medical are as follows:

HEALTH QUESTIONNAIRE

Applicants will be required to accurately answer questions regarding their medical history.

PHYSICAL EXAMINATION

Applicants will be required to successfully pass a medical examination by the Medical Officer. [a]: This includes, amongst others, the following five elements:

· Lung function test;

· Hearing test;

· Vision test (including colour vision);

· Urine test;

· Pathology test.

TIME

[b]: The entire employment medical assessment will take approximately 1½ hours to complete.

SUPPORTING MEDICAL INFORMATION

[c]: Applicants with pre-existing medical conditions are encouraged to bring medical reports, x-rays or other medical information to assist the Medical Officer in assessing their individual case.

CONFIDENTIALITY

[e]: All medical information collected as part of the medical assessment will be considered confidential, and will be released only with the specific written consent of the applicant, or in accordance with legal requirements.

Once the applicant has successfully passed the medical they will be invited to the next stage of the selection process.

Q1a. There are 5 different elements to the medical.

Answer - B (FALSE)

The passage states that, amongst others, the following five elements are examined. Therefore, there are more than five different elements to the medical and so the answer is false.

Q1b. The physical examination will take 1½ hours to complete.

Answer - C (CANNOT SAY)

The passage states it will approximately 1½ hours to complete the entire medical assessment. We cannot determine from this information how long the physical examination part of the assessment will take; therefore, the answer is cannot say from the information provided.

Q1c. Applicants with pre-existing medical conditions must bring x-rays and medical reports to assist the Medical Officer.

Answer - B (FALSE)

The passage states that applicants are 'encouraged' to bring these with them, not that they 'must'. The answer is false.

Q1d. The next stage of the selection process, upon successful completion of the medical, is the interview.

Answer - B (FALSE)

The passage confirms that the interview is conducted prior to the medical. Therefore, the correct answer is false.

Q1e. The release of confidential information collected by the Medical Officer during the medical is illegal.

Answer - B (CANNOT SAY)

The passage states that confidential information will be release only with the specific written consent of the application, or in accordance with legal requirements. This shows that there are some situations where they may be legal reasons to disclose the information. Therefore, this statement is false.

AUSTRALIAN BUSHFIRES

The summers in Australia can bring total devastation to many through the many bushfires which occur. [c]: <u>Bushfires destroy livelihoods, property, machinery, eucalyptus forests and they can even spread to the subur- ban areas of major cities.</u>

Although all bushfires can have a devastating effect, few of them fall under the 'disaster' category. [b]: <u>Some of these were in</u>:

- Victoria (2009): 173 lives were lost in this bushfire, so it is more com- monly referred to as Black Saturday.
- South Australia and Victoria (1983): This claimed 76 lives and was named Ash Wednesday.
- Southern Victoria (1969): 23 lives were claimed.
- New South Wales (1968): There were 14 fatalities in this bushfire in the Blue Mountains and coastal region.
- Hobart and Southern Tasmania (1967): 62 people were killed.
- Victoria (1939): This was named Black Friday after 71 people lost their lives.

There are two different types of bushfires in Australia - grass fires and forest fires. Grass fires more commonly occur on grazing and farm land. These often destroy fences, livestock, machinery, and they sometimes claim lives. Forest fires are largely made up of eucalyptus trees. These are extremely difficult to control due to the high amounts of flammable vapour from the leaves. [a]: <u>The bushfires are fought by large numbers of trained volunteer fire-fighters.</u> Helicopters and light aircraft are sometimes used to make observations about the fire and some also have the capacity to carry water. [d]: <u>Aircraft used to carry water in order to extinguish forest fires often find that the visibility is extremely poor. This prevents them from getting close enough to the fire in order to extinguish it with their quantities of water.</u>

Aircraft used to make observations about the fire. This includes:

- Establishing which direction the fire is travelling;

- [e]: <u>Locating suitable grid references to make fire-breaks to prevent firespread;</u>

- Locating nearby homes, businesses, other buildings and livestock that are in danger from the fire spreading.

Q2a. Bushfires are extinguished by large numbers of full-time trained fire-fighters.

Answer - B (FALSE)

The passage states that the bushfires are fought by a large number of trained volunteer fire-fighters, there is no discussion about the number of hours they do. Therefore, the statement is false.

Q2b. In total there have been 419 fatalities from Australian bushfires since 1939.

Answer - C (CANNOT SAY)

The total number of fatalities listed in the passage does equal 419. However, the passage also states that 'some of these were in' the disaster category. Therefore, we cannot confirm whether or not 419 is the total figure as there are clearly other disasters. The correct answer is cannot say based on the information provided.

Q2c. Hundreds of animals are killed by the bushfires each year.

Answer - C (CANNOT SAY)

The passage makes no reference to this claim. The passage only mentions that animals are destroyed by bushfires each year but makes no reference to numbers involved. The correct answer is cannot say based on the information provided.

Q2d. Aircraft deployed to extinguish bushfires struggle to get close to the fire due to the poor visibility.

Answer - A (TRUE)

The passage states that aircraft used to carry water in order to extinguish forest fires often find that the visibility is poor, preventing them from getting close to the fire. The correct answer is true.

Q2e. One way to prevent a bushfire from spreading is to create a fire-break.

Answer - A (TRUE)

This statement is true. The passage states: "Locating suitable grid references to make fire-breaks to prevent firespread".

AVIEMORE RAIL INCIDENT

The time is 6:37pm on Sunday the 7th of February 2010. A two-car diesel multiple unit, which has been travelling on the west Highland Line in Scotland heading towards Aviemore, has derailed and caught fire as a result. One carriage has been left in a precarious position on the 40-foot high embankment whilst the remaining three carriages have come to rest blocking both the upside and downside tracks.

[e]: In addition to blocking the lines, the incident has also caused the closure of the A35 road which is located directly below the rail line.

[b]: The train involved in the incident is a First ScotRail Class 120 Turbostar unit 156TGE. The driver of the train is a 52-year-old male named as George McDermott and the train's headcode is 6Y56. Witnesses claim that the train derailed after hitting a large boulder which had come to rest on the track following a landslide. In total, there are 34 passengers on the four carriage train. [d]: There are a number of casualties. Amongst others, an elderly female who is 72-year-old is suffering from a suspected broken collar-bone; a 32-year-old male is suffering from a serious head injury and a 21-year-old pregnant female is suffering from shock and a broken finger. The Rail Control Centre has informed all oncoming trains of the incident and has operated red stop signals along the route.

The weather is severely hampering rescue operations and the Fire and Rescue Commander has indicated that there could be a significant delay before all casualties are safely removed from the scene.

[a]: The local weather centre has forecast gales of up to 60 miles per hour over the next 12 hours with temperatures dropping to minus 3 degrees.

Q3a. The current temperature is minus 3 degrees.

Answer - B (FALSE)

The passage states the temperature will be dropping to minus 3 degrees. Therefore, the current temperature has to be higher than 3 degrees. The statement is false.

Q3b. The train involved in the incident is a First ScotRail Class 120 Turbostar unit 6Y56.

Answer - B (FALSE)

This statement is false. The passage states that "The train involved in the incident is a First ScotRail Class 120 Turbostar unit 156TGE". The difference between the two is the unit numbers supplied at the end.

Q3c. A train derailment is when the train inadvertently leaves the track.

Answer - C (CANNOT SAY)

Although this statement is factually correct, the passage makes no reference to what a derailment actually is. Therefore, the correct answer is cannot say based on the information provided.

Q3d. In total there are three passengers injured.

Answer - B (FALSE)

The passage does provide details of injuries to three passengers. However, it also states "amongst others". Therefore, the correct answer is false as there are more than three injuries in total according to the passage.

Q3e. The A35 has been affected by the incident.

Answer - A (TRUE)

The passage indicates that the incident has caused the closure of the A35 road. The statement is therefore true.

THE DEFINITION AND PURPOSE OF THE JOB

A Trainee Probation Officer is an employee of the Probation Area, appointed on a time-limited (normally two-year) contract, who is working to obtain a Diploma in Probation Studies (DipPS). Upon successful completion of training and the award of the DipPS, a Trainee Probation Officer will be eligible for appointment as a Probation Officer.

THE MAIN DUTIES AND RESPONSIBILITIES

[d]: As a person in training, the Trainee Probation Officer's principal objective is to undertake the academic work and gain the experience in probation practice necessary to acquire, practise and demonstrate the knowledge, skills, values and competencies required to obtain both the degree and the NVQ, which together constitute the DipPS. The Trainee Probation Officer's learning needs will determine the amount and nature of the work undertaken.

[a]: In the course of their training, Trainee Probation Officers will undertake work on behalf of the employing Probation Area and will provide a service to courts, penal institutions, individual Probation Area users (or persons for whom the Probation Area has a responsibility) and local communities. A Trainee Probation Officer will, therefore, be required at all times to work in accordance with the Probation Rules, National Standards, the Probation Board's policies and all other relevant enactments and policies. [e]: In particular, in all their work, Trainee Probation Officers will ensure that service delivery reflects the Probation Area's Equality of Opportunities and Anti-Discrinatory policies and will promote, especially by contributing to risk assessment and management, the Area's overriding responsibility to ensure the safety of service users, staff and the public.

Specifically, a Trainee Probation Officer will:

- [c]: Attend all required academic teaching events, as arranged by the University, the Consortium or the Probation Area.

- Complete the required academic assignments.

- Observe and participate in training and other learning experiences as arranged by the Consortium or the Probation Area.

- [b]: Undertake such work on the Probation Area's behalf as may be required.

Q4a. NVQ stands for 'National Vocational Qualification'.

Answer - C (CANNOT SAY)

Yes, NVQ does stand for National Vocational Qualification. However, the passage makes no reference to this fact. Therefore, the correct answer must be cannot say based on the information provided.

Q4b. Trainee Probation Officers will carry out work on behalf of the employing Probation Area during their training.

Answer - A (TRUE)

The passage clearly indicates that in the course of their training, Trainee Probation Officers will undertake work on behalf of the employing Probation Area. The statement is therefore true.

Q4c. During training a Trainee Probation Officer may miss some academic teaching events.

Answer - B (FALSE)

The passage states that Trainee Probation Officers will attend all academic teaching events. The statement is false based on the information provided in the passage.

Q4d. The main goal of the Trainee Probation Officer is to carry out he necessary work and gain sufficient experience in order to obtain the degree and NVQ that forms part of the DipPS.

Answer - A (TRUE)

The passage confirms that the principal objective of a Trainee Probation Officer is to undertake the academic work and gain the experience in probation practice necessary to acquire, practise and demonstrate the knowledge, skills, values and competencies required to obtain both the degree and the NVQ, which together constitute the DipPS. Therefore, the statement is true.

Q4e. Trainee Probation Officers must ensure that the service they deliver is representative of the Probation Area's equality policy.

Answer - A (TRUE)

The passage clearly states that Trainee Probation Officers will ensure that service delivery reflects the Probation Area's Equality of Opportunities and Anti-Discriminatory policies. The correct answer is true.

ACCOUNT BILLING INFORMATION

There are two separate options offered for account billing:

Monthly* - This option operates on a 4-week cycle beginning on the day of account activation.

Annual - This option operates on a 365-day cycle beginning on the day of account activation.

Note: *Customers on a monthly billing cycle are billed every 4 weeks.

[a]: When your account reaches its appropriate billing day (your account's expiration date) your credit card will be automatically billed for the next billing cycle and [d]: your account expiration date will be extended by an additional 4 weeks (or 365 for annual packages) and you will receive a receipt via email. If the transaction is unsuccessful for any reason, we will attempt to re-bill your credit card for 2 consecutive days and send an unsuccessful renewal email for each unsuccessful attempt (to your accounts specified Billing Profile email address).

After your first unsuccessful renewal attempt your account status will be updated to Billing Hold Level 1. This status indicates that your account is overdue but otherwise has no direct effect on your service which will continue for up to 4 weeks following your actual expiration date.

4 WEEKS PAST ACCOUNT EXPIRATION

[b]: 4 weeks after your account expires we will attempt to re-bill your credit card for two monthly payments. If successful your account expiration date will be extended by an additional 4 weeks (from bill date) and you will receive a receipt via email. If unsuccessful your account status will be updated to Billing Hold Level 2. This status indicates that your account is now more than 4 weeks overdue and we will close all account service until payment has been received. We will attempt to re-bill your credit card for 2 consecutive days and send an unsuccessful renewal email for each unsuccessful attempt.

When your account is in this status you will still be able to log in and access both the Earn Cash page (to manage affiliate referrals) and the Renew Account page.

56 DAYS PAST ACCOUNT EXPIRATION

56 days after your account expires we will attempt to re-bill your credit card for three monthly payments. If successful your account expiration date will be extended by an additional 4 weeks (from bill date), your account will be reactivated and you will receive a receipt via email. If unsuccessful your account will be permanently closed.

Q5a. The account's expiration date can be determined as the billing day.

Answer - A (TRUE)

The passage confirms that the billing day is also known as the account's expiration date. Therefore, the statement is true.

Q5b. Billing Hold Level 2 occurs when an attempt to take two monthly payments after an account is 4 weeks past account expiration fails.

Answer - A (TRUE)

The passage makes it clear that 4 weeks after the account expires they will attempt to re-bill the credit card for two monthly payments. It also goes on to state that if the transaction is unsuccessful the status will be updated to Billing Hold Level 2. The statement is therefore true based on this information.

Q5c. Customers who opt for the monthly billing option will be billed every 4 weeks on the first day of each month.

Answer - C (CANNOT SAY)

This is a difficult one! The passage states that the monthly billing option "operates on a 4-week cycle beginning on the day of account activation".

You could be forgiven for selecting false as your answer. However, because we do not know for sure which day each customer has activated their account, we cannot confirm that any of them will be billed on any other day than the first of each month. Whilst it is highly unlikely that all customers will have signed up on the first day of each month, we cannot say for certain this is the case. Therefore, based on the information provided we must select cannot say as the correct answer.

Q5d. For the annual billing option the first expiration date will be 365 days after account activation.

Answer - A (TRUE)

The passage states that the expiration date for annual billing option is 365 days. The correct answer is true.

Q5e. Billing Hold Level 1 occurs after the first successful renewal attempt.

Answer - B (FALSE)

The correct answer is false. Billing Hold Level 1 occurs after the first unsuccessful renewal attempt, not successful.

Congratulations on reaching this far in the guide! Now move on to the final mock exam and let's see how much you have improved since the start.

VERBAL
REASONING
FINAL MOCK EXAM

During the final mock exam there are 12 practice passages which each contain 5 questions. Answer each question based solely on the information provided. You must select either TRUE, FALSE or CANNOT SAY based on the information provided in the passage.

- You have 12 minutes to complete the entire mock exam.

- Concentrate fully on each test.

- If unsure of an answer you should select the one that you believe to be correct.

- Avoid all forms of wild guessing.

Once you have completed the exam check your answers with the ones that are provided at the end.

VERBAL REASONING
FINAL MOCK EXAM

Number of Passages = 12

Questions per Passage = 5

Total Number of Questions = 60

Surname:

Forename:

Date of Test (dd/mm/yyyy):

Allotted Time = 12 Minutes

FACTS ABOUT ANTARCTICA

Very few people ever travel to Antarctica, which is one of the seven continents on the Earth. The reason is because Antarctica is so cold and icy that it is a very inhospitable place for human life. It is a very fascinating place, with lots of amazing wildlife in the surrounding waters.

Some of the many interesting facts about Antarctica include:

- Antarctica, along with the Arctic, is one of the two coldest places on Earth. It is located very close to the South Pole, while the Arctic is to the north.

- One third of all the fresh water on the entire planet is located on Antarctica.

- The temperature rarely gets above freezing, so that the entire area is covered in ice and snow. In fact, the ice and snow is one mile deep in most spots and in some areas it is up to three miles deep.

- Very few creatures live on the actual land; in fact the largest creature that resides directly on Antarctica is the midge. Midges are only half an inch long. There are many living creatures in the water surrounding the land, however.

- The lowest temperature ever recorded on Antarctica was in 1983. It was -129 degrees Fahrenheit.

- No single country has claimed ownership over Antarctica. In fact, all of the countries have agreed to joint ownership and everyone is able to send scientific research missions to the area.

- No native people reside on the land, as it would be near impossible for humans to live there for an extended period of time.

- Many people think of Antarctica as a place where it snows continuously, when it fact it rarely snows each year. Instead, the appearance of snowstorms is caused by existing snow that blows off of the ground by hard winds.

- For a large part of the history of the Earth, Antarctica was a warm continent.

While people do not reside on this ice cold land, some people do go there for research projects and other exploratory missions. It is a vast and beautiful land and much of its beauty is because it is untouched by industrialisation and the damage that humans can inflict.

Q1a. Antarctica is owned by a single country.

A - TRUE	B - FALSE	C - CANNOT SAY

Q1b. The temperature on Antarctica sometimes rises above freezing.

A - TRUE	B - FALSE	C - CANNOT SAY

Q1c. It is impossible for humans to live on Antarctica for long periods of time.

A - TRUE	B - FALSE	C - CANNOT SAY

Q1d. Antarctica is yet to be affected by industrialisation.

A - TRUE	B - FALSE	C - CANNOT SAY

Q1e. The Arctic is one of the coldest places on Earth.

A - TRUE	B - FALSE	C - CANNOT SAY

THE QUALITIES OF A GOOD TEACHER

There is no question that teaching is one of the most important careers in the UK. Our teachers are helping to shape the future of our population, as they are training our children to enter the workforce and become the leaders of tomorrow. Without teachers there would be no formal education for our youth in the UK. Many people want to be a teacher, but a large number find that it is just not for them. Not just anyone can be a good teacher, because it takes certain qualities and personality traits to teach children of all ages.

Those who are the best teachers often have certain aspects to their personalities that enable them to command the attention and respect of their students. Some of the qualities that make up a good teacher include:

- Patience - Patience is by far the most vital aspect of a teacher's personality. In order to keep calm and cool when children are misbehaving, a teacher must have extreme patience. This is important when handling younger children, as they can often be difficult to control.

- Intelligence - Of course, in order for a teacher to properly instruct their students, they must be well-versed in the subject that they are teaching. They must be able to give their students the right information and to be prepared to answer any questions that their pupils may come up with.

- Creativity - In order to make lessons more interesting and to engage the students, a teacher must use creativity. Good teachers are able to think of clever ways to present the materials that need to be learned so that children actually want to learn.

- Organisation - Teachers must be organised, as they have a lot of things that they must juggle. They have to keep track of the lessons that they have taught and what they have coming up. They have to keep a hold on papers that they need to grade and they also must have all of the necessary hand-outs for each of their classes.

- Leadership – Teachers are required to lead their pupils. They must be able to stand in front of the classroom with confidence, so that the children trust and respect them and are willing to be led.

Being a teacher is one of the hardest careers in the world and being good at it is even more challenging. A good teacher will be able to demonstrate all of the above qualities on a daily basis.

Q2a. In total there are five different qualities that make up a good teacher.

A - TRUE	B - FALSE	C - CANNOT SAY

Q2b. Patience is not the most important attribute of a teacher's personality.

A - TRUE	B - FALSE	C - CANNOT SAY

Q2c. Most people find that teaching is not for them.

A - TRUE	B - FALSE	C - CANNOT SAY

Q2d. Teaching is not a particularly well paid job.

A - TRUE	B - FALSE	C - CANNOT SAY

Q2e. Younger children are often the easiest to control.

A - TRUE	B - FALSE	C - CANNOT SAY

THE EVOLUTION OF MAN

Evolution is a widely studied science that many scientific leaders have researched and pondered over for many years. For the most part, these scientists believe that human beings evolved from Order Primates. This group includes chimpanzees, monkeys, gorillas and lemurs. They have gathered their information by studying fossils that have been unearthed from all over the world, with the oldest dating back more than 5 million years ago. Humans evolved because of diet and environmental factors, among other things. Many stages of man have been identified and here we will explain each of them.

The earliest stage of man included such species as Australopithecus anamensis, Australopithecus robustus, Australopithecus africanus and Australopithecus boisei. Australopithecus anamensis is identified as a species that walked on two feet. Australopithecus africanus had a larger brain than other species at the time and seemed to have developed molars and canine teeth, as did the Australopithecus robustus, indicating that both ate things that required more chewing and grinding than before.

Then came along Homo habilis. This species had a much larger brain size than the Australopithecus, which enabled the species to invent tools that they could use for making things and killing prey. Homo habilis may have been able to speak and was about 5 feet tall and weighed around 100 lbs.

The next species to come along was Homo erectus, who had an even larger brain size than Hobo habilis. Erectus was also taller (about 5 feet 5 inches) and this is attributed to the fact that he was smarter and able to hunt for meat. The meat made Erectus grow larger and stronger.

Homo sapiens (Archaic) were next in the evolution of man. Fossils have been found all over the world and scientists can determine from these that he had an even larger brain, which enabled him to reason, speak, make plans and control how he moved his body. He is believed to have been a socialised being that used various weapons and tools.

Homo sapiens neanderthalensis were the next evolution of man, leading to our species today. This species appeared at the very end of the ice age and they were able to survive in very cold weather, because of their body size, which retained more body heat. They had even more social skills than the species before them, as well as a very strong and muscular build. The evolution of man was a long process, over approximately 5 million years, which resulted in the humans that reside on Earth today.

Q3a. Homo erectus evolved prior to Homo habilis.

A - TRUE	B - FALSE	C - CANNOT SAY

Q3b. Homo sapiens were capable of controlling their own body movement.

A - TRUE	B - FALSE	C - CANNOT SAY

Q3c. The human race is more than 5 million years old.

A - TRUE	B - FALSE	C - CANNOT SAY

Q3d. Homo habilis was able to speak.

A - TRUE	B - FALSE	C - CANNOT SAY

Q3e. Homo erectus was capable of eating meat.

A - TRUE	B - FALSE	C - CANNOT SAY

THE DIFFERENCE BETWEEN AFFECT AND EFFECT

Not everyone is skilled with grammar and even those who are struggle with some of the most commonly mistaken words in the English language. Two words that cause a lot of confusion for people are affect and effect. Many people have a lot of trouble with the usage and the meanings of these words, as they are very easy to mix up. The majority of people aren't really sure of when to use one or the other, which is why they simply end up guessing.

The reason why these two words are so confusing is that while each is a different part of speech, they sometimes function as other parts of speech. In most cases, affect is a verb and effect is a noun. You can affect something, which will produce an effect on that thing. Things are always affected, never effected. This is the general rule that you should always remember. Only in rare cases will affect or effect serve as different parts of speech. Remember that an effect is always something that is produced and an affect is what you do to something.

Just to be thoroughly confusing, there are very rare situations when effect will be used as a verb and affect will be used as a noun. For the most part, you will never have to use them in these cases. Use the general rule from above (affect is a verb and effect is a noun), but try to remember the following odd instances. As a verb, effect means to accomplish, produce or execute something. As a noun, affect is used by psychologists to refer to desires and emotions as factors in how someone acts or thinks. Obviously, both of these instances do not occur often, but you will see them sometimes in things you may be reading, such as an academic journal. Always keep in your mind that under most circumstances, 'affect' is a verb and 'effect' is a noun.

Q4a. In most cases, effect is a verb and affect is a noun.

A - TRUE	B - FALSE	C - CANNOT SAY

Q4b. If something is affected there will be a resultant effect on it.

A - TRUE	B - FALSE	C - CANNOT SAY

Q4c. There are occasions when effect will be used as a verb and affect will be used as a noun.

A - TRUE	B - FALSE	C - CANNOT SAY

Q4d. Affect can be described as what you do to something.

A - TRUE	B - FALSE	C - CANNOT SAY

Q4e. Affect is always something that is produced and an effect is what you do to something.

A - TRUE	B - FALSE	C - CANNOT SAY

MOUNT EVEREST

Mount Everest is one of the most famous natural landmarks in the world; it is the highest point above sea level on Earth. Many mountain climbers seek to climb Mount Everest as their ultimate goal and people visit in droves every single year to test their climbing skills on this peak. Here are some facts about Mount Everest to help you understand more about the mountain and its history.

· Everest is about 29,000 feet above sea level.

· The mountain was actually named by British surveyors for George Everest. He was a famous Surveyor General of India throughout the mid-nineteenth century.

· Everest has been altered considerably by five major glaciers, which still continue to change how the mountain looks. Glaciers have been credited with turning the mountain into a massive pyramid with three large ridges and three faces. The best time to climb Everest is at the beginning of May. This will ensure that the monsoon season is avoided.

· In 1975, the largest expedition to climb Everest was completed. A group of 410 people from China scaled the mountain together.

· One of the biggest problems that people face when climbing Everest is the extreme climate. The temperatures on the mountain never get above freezing and in the dead of winter they are well within negative temperatures. Climbers have to prepare not only for the lack of oxygen at altitude, but also for the incredibly cold temperatures.

· Everest is rising 1/3 of an inch every single year. It is also very slowly moving northeastward, at about 3 inches per year.

· Climbers Peter Habeler and Reinhold Messner have the distinction of being the first people to climb the mountain without supplemental oxygen. They did this in 1978.

· The safest year for climbers on Mount Everest was 1993. This is because 129 climbers made it all the way to the summit, with 8 deaths.

· 1996 is considered the least safe year on the mountain. 98 climbers made it to the summit, yet 15 died.

· The mountain is considered very sacred by those in Tibet and Nepal. In Tibet, Mount Everest is called Chomolangma, which means 'Goddess Mother of Snows', in the Tibetan language. Those in Nepal refer to the mountain as Sagarmatha, which means 'Mother of the Universe'.

Q5a. The monsoon season starts after the month of May.

A - TRUE	B - FALSE	C - CANNOT SAY

Q5b. Everest is increasing in height each year.

A - TRUE	B - FALSE	C - CANNOT SAY

Q5c. To some people in Nepal, Mount Everest is also called Chomolangma, which means 'Goddess Mother of Snows'.

A - TRUE	B - FALSE	C - CANNOT SAY

Q5d. Everest is the tallest mountain in the world.

A - TRUE	B - FALSE	C - CANNOT SAY

Q5e. George Everest worked in India during the mid-nineteenth century.

A - TRUE	B - FALSE	C - CANNOT SAY

THE CAMINO DE SANTIAGO

The Camino de Santiago is a major Christian pilgrimage route to the Cathedral of Santiago de Compostela in northwestern Spain. It dates back to medieval times and is still in existence today. This historic pilgrimage route has many interesting and unique things about it. Here are some facts and figures related to the Camino de Santiago:

- In English, The Camino de Santiago means The way of Saint James, which is how many in the English-speaking world refer to this historic route.
- The Camino has been a Christian route for more than 1,000 years and many believe that it was used for other purposes long before that.
- The Camino was named as the very first European Cultural Route in 1987 by the Council of Europe. It is also one of UNESCO's world Heritage Sites.
- The symbol of the Camino de Santiago is the scallop shell. There are differing stories as to why, but many believe it is because the shell has multiple grooves that come together at a single point. This is a metaphor for how people came down many paths to end up at the Camino de Santiago.
- The earliest records of visitors to the Cathedral date back all the way to the 8th century.
- Pilgrims who travelled the route purchased a "credencial", or pilgrim's passport, from the Spanish government so that they could safely travel the route. They could show their passport at various pilgrim's hostels along the way in Spain and France, where they could stay overnight.
- Pilgrims who completed the walk along the Camino de Santiago were given a certificate of accomplishment called the Compostela. They had to walk at least 100 km in order to achieve this, but it was a very big honour for the devout people that had travelled to the Cathedral.
- Every day at noon, a pilgrim's mass is held at the Cathedral of Santiago de Compostela in honour of the pilgrims.
- On special Holy Years, more pilgrims than ever take the route. The last Holy Year was 2010, when more than 272,000 pilgrims walked the route to the Cathedral. The next Holy Year is in 2021. Holy Years are when the sacred holiday of Saint James's Day (July 25), falls on a Sunday.
- The Camino de Santiago is a very famous and historical route that people today still travel to get to the Cathedral of Santiago de Compostela.

Q6a. The people who walk the Camino de Santiago are known as pilgrims.

A - TRUE	B - FALSE	C - CANNOT SAY

Q6b. The next Holy Year will be 2012.

A - TRUE	B - FALSE	C - CANNOT SAY

Q6c. The Camino de Santiago is 100 km long.

A - TRUE	B - FALSE	C - CANNOT SAY

Q6d. A credencial is a pilgrim's passport that enables them to travel safely.

A - TRUE	B - FALSE	C - CANNOT SAY

Q6e. People have been walking the Camino de Santiago since the 8th century.

A - TRUE	B - FALSE	C - CANNOT SAY

THE EUROPEAN UNION

The European Union was officially established in 1993 under its current name. The history of the EU and its current actions are something that many people are not fully aware of. Here are some interesting facts and figures about the European Union.

- The Maastricht Treaty of 1993 formally named the European Union.
- The EU traces its roots all the way back to the European Coal and Steel Community and the European Economic Community, formed together by six member countries in 1958.
- The EU has a combined population of 500 million inhabitants in 27 member states. This is 7.3% of the world's population.
- The eurozone, which is a monetary union within the European Union, was established in 1999. There are 17 member states (countries) in the eurozone, all of which utilise the euro as their form of currency. This enables free spending in all of the eurozone countries without having to exchange currencies, making movement from country to country much easier.
- There are many important institutions of the EU, such as the European Commission, Council of the European Union, the European Council, the European Central Bank, and the Court Justice of the European Union.
- European Parliament is part of the legislative function of the EU and members are directly elected from each member country every 5 years.
- The anthem of the European Union is "Ode to Joy".
- In the entire organisation there are 23 different languages spoken.
- The euro currency was introduced on January 1, 2002, where it was printed and distributed throughout 12 member countries. This was a huge logistical operation, with nearly 80 billion coins involved.
- 38,000 people are employed by the European Commission.
- 1% of the annual budget of the EU is spent on staff and administration, as well as continued maintenance on buildings.
- The European Commission is hailed as having one of the largest translation centres in the world, with 1,750 linguists. There are also 600 support staff members for the linguists.
- European Parliament holds its regular committee meetings in Brussels.
- The EU has the world's third largest population, after China and India.
- The EU's GDP is now bigger than that of the US.

The European Union has certainly grown immensely since it was officially named in 1993. 12 member states were added since 2004 and the population and economic impact continues to grow.

Q7a. There are currently 12 countries using the euro currency.

A - TRUE	B - FALSE	C - CANNOT SAY

Q7b. There are more people living in the European Union than China.

A - TRUE	B - FALSE	C - CANNOT SAY

Q7c. 7.3% of the world's population live in the European Union.

A - TRUE	B - FALSE	C - CANNOT SAY

Q7d. Greece is in the European Union.

A - TRUE	B - FALSE	C - CANNOT SAY

Q7e. One of the benefits of the eurozone is that it negates the need to change currency between the different countries that form part of it.

A - TRUE	B - FALSE	C - CANNOT SAY

RULES OF AMERICAN FOOTBALL

American football is an incredibly popular sport all over the United States, but it is less popular throughout other countries. An increasing number of people in the UK are starting to play and watch this classic American sport. If you want to be able to play, or understand the sport while watching it on television, you need to know the rules. Here is an overview of the basic rules of American football.

OFFENSE AND DEFENSE

Each team has 11 players on the field at one time. The team that has possession of the football is the offense, and their objective is to advance the ball down the field. They do this by running with the ball, or passing it to another team-mate. They score points when they get to the very end of the field, crossing the goal line into the end zone. The team that does not have the ball is the defense. Their objective is to prevent the other team from getting into the end zone and scoring a touchdown. They do this by attempting to block players from catching passes, tackling players who are running with the ball, and/or trying to catch passes that are intended for the offensive team (catching such a pass is called an interception).

If the offensive team scores, or if they lose possession of the ball to the defense, then the two teams switch roles. This continues on until the four timed quarters of the game have been completed. The game is divided into four 15-minute quarters, along with a half-time break of 12 minutes. The teams change ends of the field after each quarter.

THE FIELD

A football field measures 100 yards long and is 53 yards wide. There are markers on the field to tell the players, coaches and officials which yard line they are on. Every 10 yards is marked by a line. The end zone is also marked and is at the 0-yard line on the field. This zone is 10 yards long, but does not count towards the 100 yards of the field.

SCORING

If the offense makes it to the end zone, they score a touchdown, which is six points. They can then either kick a field goal for an extra point, or they can do a small play in the last 10 yards of the field which is called a two-point conversion and is worth two points. If they do not score a touchdown and decide to try for a field goal, they can score three points. There are many other intricate rules of American football, but the above are all of the most important aspects.

Q8a. In American Football you can only score points when the ball crosses the goal line into the end zone via a touchdown.

A - TRUE	B - FALSE	C - CANNOT SAY

Q8b. When a team does not have the ball they are the defense.

A - TRUE	B - FALSE	C - CANNOT SAY

Q8c. The game of American Football, excluding breaks, is 60 minutes in duration.

A - TRUE	B - FALSE	C - CANNOT SAY

Q8d. The protective helmets worn by American Footballers are designed to protect the head from injury.

A - TRUE	B - FALSE	C - CANNOT SAY

Q8e. A football field measures 100 yards wide and 53 yards long.

A - TRUE	B - FALSE	C - CANNOT SAY

FACTS ABOUT THE NATIONAL GEOGRAPHIC

The National Geographic Society (NGS) is a group that is headquartered in Washington, DC in the United States, which publishes a magazine titled National Geographic. The group and the fascinating magazine it releases are very interesting to many people all over the world, as they have made huge strides in environmental and historical preservation, among other things.

- The National Geographic Society was founded on January 27, 1888 by Gardiner Greene Hubbard.

- Worldwide membership of the society is currently at about 8.5 million people.

- The logo for the NGS is a rectangular yellow portrait frame, which can be found as its television logo and on the margins surrounding the front cover of their magazine.

- The organisation is designed to fund research and preservation of historical, archaeological, and natural science areas throughout the entire world. It is a non-profit organisation.

- The Society has given grants for scientific research since it began, and recently gave out its 10,000th grant.

- The NGS began as a group for elite world travellers and academics who were wealthy and interested in advancing tourism and interest in history, science and culture.

- In 2004, the NGS headquarters in Washington, DC was one of the first buildings ever to receive a Green Certification from Global Green USA.

- The magazine started nine months after the society was founded in October 1888. It is published 12 times per year, along with at least four supplements.

- More than 50 million readers all over the world read National Geographic every month, in 32 different languages.

- NGS has funded more than 9,600 conservation, research and exploration projects throughout the entire Earth.

- In addition to the magazine, NGS reaches more than 400 million people per month through videos, their television channel, books, radio, music, films, interactive media and more.

Q9a. More than 50 million readers all over the world read National Geographic every year, in 32 different languages.

A - TRUE	B - FALSE	C - CANNOT SAY

Q9b. The National Geographic Society's magazine is not titled National Geographic.

A - TRUE	B - FALSE	C - CANNOT SAY

Q9c. The National Geographic Society has 50 million members all over the world in 32 different languages.

A - TRUE	B - FALSE	C - CANNOT SAY

Q9d. The National Geographic Society was founded over 100 years ago.

A - TRUE	B - FALSE	C - CANNOT SAY

Q9e. The National Geographic Society is a profitable business.

A - TRUE	B - FALSE	C - CANNOT SAY

INTERNAL COMBUSTION ENGINE THEORY

Internal combustion engines are the most commonly used engines in the entire world. They are used in a wide range of vehicles. The chances are if you drive a car, yours uses this type of engine. They are also used in industrial applications and largely replaced the steam engine throughout the 20th century.

WHAT IS THE THEORY?

The main principle behind any type of internal combustion engine is if you put a small amount of a type of high-energy fuel, such as gasoline, into a very small space and ignite it, a large amount of energy will be released in the form of gas that expands. This energy can then be used to propel almost anything and it is very effective. This is why the majority of common vehicle engines are built based upon this theory. This principle is the core that most car engines today are built on.

HOW IT WORKS

The engine utilises a fossil fuel inside of a combustion chamber and combines this with an oxidiser, which is usually air. When the air and the fossil fuel are heated in the combustion chamber, the gas and the air will expand. The expansion of the gas and the air when combustion is applied causes a force to the pistons, turbine blades, or nozzle inside of the engine. This then transforms the chemical energy of the internal combustion energy into mechanical energy that powers the vehicle or industrial application.

Most cars on the roads right now use a four-stroke combustion cycle. This converts gasoline so that it can propel the car forward. This is also called the 'Otto Cycle', as it is named after the inventor, Nikolaus Otto, who invented it in 1867. These four strokes are called the intake stroke, compression stroke, combustion stroke, and the exhaust stroke.

The first internal combustion engine was created by Jean Joseph Étienne Lenoir, a Belgian engineer, in 1859. Without his application of the theory, we might not have the advanced vehicle engines we have today.

Q10a. The majority of vehicle engines are built based upon the internal combustion engine theory.

A - TRUE	B - FALSE	C - CANNOT SAY

Q10b. The first internal combustion engine was built in Belgium.

A - TRUE	B - FALSE	C - CANNOT SAY

Q10c. Without the internal combustion engine we would not have the motor vehicle.

A - TRUE	B - FALSE	C - CANNOT SAY

Q10d. Gas and air expansion in the combustion chamber occurs when air and fossil fuel are heated.

A - TRUE	B - FALSE	C - CANNOT SAY

Q10e. Internal combustion engines replaced the steam engine in the 20th century.

A - TRUE	B - FALSE	C - CANNOT SAY

HOW A FRIDGE WORKS

Refrigerators are widely popular everywhere in the world and they are a vital part of any kitchen. If you want to be able to keep food fresh and chilled to the correct temperature, you will need one of these appliances. Not only are they useful, there are also attractive and innovative models that add to the aesthetic appeal of your kitchen. You probably see your fridge multiple times per day but are unaware how it works.

PARTS OF A FRIDGE

To understand how a fridge works, first you have to know what parts are inside of it. Every refrigerator has five main components that help it to keep your food and drinks cold.

THE COOLING PROCESS

When you turn on your fridge, it does not automatically become cold. There are intricate processes at work inside of the appliance. The first thing that happens when your fridge is turned on is that the refrigerant liquid, which is contained within the coils, is compressed into a gas by the compressor. The gas will heat up as it becomes pressurised. The exterior heat-exchange pipes that reside on the rear panel of the unit then lose heat as the hot refrigerant gas dissipates it. The gas will then condense into liquid when it is under this high pressure. This pressurised refrigerant liquid will flow through the expansion valve, which is essentially a very tiny hole. One side of the hole will have the high-pressure liquid, while the other side will have the low-pressure gas that the compressor is pulling from.

Once the liquid flows through the expansion valve, which is essential to the running of the fridge, it will start to boil and turn into a vapour, which drops its temperature. This will cool down the refrigerator. The cold refrigerant gas will then go back through the compressor and the entire process will be repeated.

Q11a. Exterior heat-exchanging pipes are located externally on the rear panel.

A - TRUE	B - FALSE	C - CANNOT SAY

Q11b. Fridges are commonly known as 'white goods'.

A - TRUE	B - FALSE	C - CANNOT SAY

Q11c. In total there are five components to the fridge.

A - TRUE	B - FALSE	C - CANNOT SAY

Q11d. Without the expansion valve the fridge will not operate correctly.

A - TRUE	B - FALSE	C - CANNOT SAY

Q11e. The refrigerant liquid becomes a gas.

A - TRUE	B - FALSE	C - CANNOT SAY

HOW AN AEROPLANES FLIES

There are three principles that you have to understand in order to fully grasp how an aeroplane is able to fly and how it does this effectively. Getting to know The Bernouilli Effect, The Coanda Effect and Newton's Third Law will help you to understand how an aeroplane flies.

THE BERNOUILLI EFFECT

The Bernouilli Effect explains how the wings enable the aeroplane to fly. The wings are curved into a specific shape to make what is called an air- foil. On the majority of aircrafts, the bottom of the wing (or airfoil) is flat, while the top is a more curved surface. Air will flow very fast over the top because of the shape, which thins this air considerably. This thinner air at the top of the airfoil creates a strong vacuum, which pulls up on the wing. This is how the lifting action is generated and this keeps the aeroplane in the sky.

THE COANDA EFFECT

The Coanda Effect is another force that helps to keep the plane in the air. This is a principle of physics that says that a jet of fluid will most often tend to follow along a curved surface. This is another important factor in keeping the curved wings and body of the plane in the air.

NEWTON'S THIRD LAW

Newton's Third Law explains another reason why an aeroplane will fly. The trailing edge of the wing curves in a downward fashion, so that when air flows over this, it will angle in a downward motion off the wing and shoot out fast behind it. Newton's Third Law of thermodynamics is a principle in physics. It explains that for any action that occurs, there is an opposite and equal reaction to it. As the wing pushes downward and forces are behind it, the air will push the wing upwards. This principle, along with The Bernouilli Effect, explains how an aeroplane will stay in the air. Essentially, it is because of the advanced design of the wings and the body of the plane.

Q12a. Millions of people fly on aeroplanes each year.

| A - TRUE | B - FALSE | C - CANNOT SAY |

Q12b. Newton's Third Law is named so because it is the third law in the process of flight.

| A - TRUE | B - FALSE | C - CANNOT SAY |

Q12c. The air flow over the top of a wing is faster than the air flow underneath the wing.

| A - TRUE | B - FALSE | C - CANNOT SAY |

Q12d. The wings on an aeroplane are curved so that the air can flow faster over them.

| A - TRUE | B - FALSE | C - CANNOT SAY |

Q12e. The body of a plane has nothing to do with the aeroplane staying in the air.

| A - TRUE | B - FALSE | C - CANNOT SAY |

Great work! You have now completed the mock exam. Let's now see how well you have done by checking your answers.

ANSWERS AND EXPLANATIONS TO VERBAL REASONING FINAL MOCK EXAM

FACTS ABOUT ANTARCTICA

Very few people ever travel to Antarctica, which is one of the seven continents on the Earth. The reason is because Antarctica is so cold and icy that it is a very inhospitable place for human life. It is a very fascinating place, with lots of amazing wildlife in the surrounding waters.

Some of the many interesting facts about Antarctica include:

- [e]: <u>Antarctica, along with the arctic, is one of the two coldest places on Earth.</u> It is located very close to the South Pole, while the Arctic is to the north.

- One third of all the fresh water on the entire planet is located on Antarctica.

- There are absolutely no trees on this icy continent.

- [b]: <u>The temperature rarely gets above freezing, so that the entire area is covered in ice and snow.</u> In fact, the ice and snow is one mile deep in most spots and in some areas it is up to three miles deep.

- The lowest temperature ever recorded on Antarctica was in 1983. It was -129 degrees Fahrenheit.

- Codfish in the waters surrounding Antarctica actually have antifreeze flowing through their blood because the water is so cold.

- [a]: <u>No single country has claimed ownership over Antarctica.</u> In fact, all of the countries have agreed to joint ownership and everyone is able to send scientific research missions to the area. [3]: <u>No native people reside on the land, as it would be near impossible for humans to live there for an extended period of time.</u>

- Many people think of Antarctica as a place where it snows continuously, when it fact it rarely snows each year. Instead, the appearance of snowstorms is caused by existing snow that blows off of the ground by hard winds.

- For a large part of the history of the Earth, Antarctica was a warm continent.

While people do not reside on this ice cold land, some people do go there for research projects and other exploratory missions. [d]: <u>It is a vast and beautiful land and much of its beauty is because it is untouched by industrialisation and the damage that humans can inflict.</u>

Q1a. Antarctica is owned by a single country.

Answer - B (FALSE)

The passage states that no single country has claimed ownership of Antarctica; therefore, this statement is false.

Q1b. The temperature on Antarctica sometimes rises above freezing.

Answer - A (TRUE)

The passage informs us that "The temperature rarely gets above freezing…" Because of this fact we can accurately state that the temperature does, at some point, rise above freezing. Therefore, the statement is true.

Q1c. It is impossible for humans to live on Antarctica for long periods of time.

Answer - B (FALSE)

The passage states it would be "near impossible for humans to live there for an extended period of time". If something is near to being impossible, it cannot be impossible. The statement is false based on the information provided in the passage.

Q1d. Antarctica is yet to be affected by industrialisation.

Answer - A (TRUE)

The passage clearly states that Antarctica is "untouched by industrialisation". The statement is true.

Q1e. The Arctic is one of the coldest places on Earth.

Answer - A (TRUE)

The passage states that "Antarctica, along with the Arctic, is one of the two coldest places on Earth". Therefore, the statement is true.

THE QUALITIES OF A GOOD TEACHER

There is no question that teaching is one of the most important careers in the UK. Our teachers are helping to shape the future of our population, as they are training our children to enter the workforce and become the leaders of tomorrow. Without teachers there would be no formal education for our youth in the UK. [c]: <u>Many people want to be a teacher, but a large number find that it is just not for them.</u> Not just anyone can be a good teacher, because it takes certain qualities and personality traits to teach children of all ages.

Those who are the best teachers often have certain aspects to their personalities that enable them to command the attention and respect of their students. [a]: <u>Some of the qualities that make up a good teacher include:</u>

- Patience - [b]: <u>Patience is by far the most vital aspect of a teacher's personality.</u> In order to keep calm and cool when children are misbehaving, a teacher must have extreme patience. [e]: <u>This is important when handling younger children, as they can often be difficult to control.</u>

- Intelligence - Of course, in order for a teacher to properly instruct their students, they must be well-versed in the subject that they are teaching. They must be able to give their students the right information and to be prepared to answer any questions that their pupils may come up with.

- Creativity - In order to make lessons more interesting and to engage the students, a teacher must use creativity. Good teachers are able to think of clever ways to present the materials that need to be learned so that children actually want to learn.

- Organisation - Teachers must be organised, as they have a lot of things that they must juggle. They have to keep track of the lessons that they have taught and what they have coming up. They have to keep a hold on papers that they need to grade and they also must have all of the necessary hand-outs for each of their classes.

- Leadership – Teachers are required to lead their pupils. They must be able to stand in front of the classroom with confidence, so that the children trust and respect them and are willing to be led.

Being a teacher is one of the hardest careers in the world and being good at it is even more challenging. A good teacher will be able to demonstrate all of the above qualities on a daily basis.

Q2a. In total there are five different qualities that make up a good teacher.

Answer - B (FALSE)

The passage states that "Some of the qualities that make up a good teacher include…". Because the sentence in the passage states 'some of the qualities include, this suggests that there more than five qualities. Therefore, the statement is false.

Q2b. Patience is not the most important attribute of a teacher's personality.

Answer - B (FALSE)

The passage confirms that patience is the most vital aspect of a teacher's personality. The statement is false.

Q2c. Most people find that teaching is not for them.

Answer - C (CANNOT SAY)

The passage states that "Many people want to be a teacher, but a large number find that it is just not for them". The statement makes reference to most people. The passage just states that a large number find it is not for them. We cannot decide from the information in the passage whether a large number is 'most ' people, therefore, the correct answer is cannot say.

Q2d. Teaching is not a particularly well paid job.

Answer - C (CANNOT SAY)

The passage does not make any reference to this claim. The correct answer is cannot say based on the information in the passage.

Q2e. Younger children are often the easiest to control.

Answer - C (CANNOT SAY)

The passage states that younger children can often be difficult to control. You could, therefore, be forgiven for selecting false as the correct answer. In fact, if the question stated – "Younger children are often easier to control". The answer would be false.

However, the statement asks us to consider whether or not "Younger children are often the easiest to control". There is no information con- tained in the passage that will help us to confirm that younger children are the easiest to control; therefore, the correct answer must be 'cannot say'. There is a difference between 'easiest' and 'easier'.

THE EVOLUTION OF MAN

Evolution is a widely studied science that many scientific leaders have researched and pondered over for many years. <u>ᶜ: For the most part, these scientists believe that human beings evolved from Order Primates.</u> This group includes chimpanzees, monkeys, gorillas and lemurs. They have gathered their information by studying fossils that have been unearthed from all over the world, with the oldest dating back more than 5 million years ago. Humans evolved because of diet and environmental factors, among other things. Many stages of man have been identified and here we will explain each of them.

The earliest stage of man included such species as Australopithecus anamensis, Australopithecus robustus, Australopithecus africanus and Australopithecus boisei. Australopithecus anamensis is identified as a species that walked on two feet. Australopithecus africanus had a larger brain than other species at the time and seemed to have developed molars and canine teeth, as did the Australopithecus robustus, indicating that both ate things that required more chewing and grinding than before.

Then came along Homo habilis. This species had a much larger brain size than the Australopithecus, which enabled the species to invent tools that they could use for making things and killing prey. Homo habilis may have been able to speak and was about 5 feet tall and weighed around 100 lbs.

ᵃ: <u>The next species to come along was Homo erectus, who had an even larger brain size than Hobo habilis.</u> ᵉ: <u>Erectus was also taller (about 5 feet 5 inches) and this is attributed to the fact that he was smarter and able to hunt for meat.</u> The meat made Erectus grow larger and stronger.

Homo sapiens (Archaic) were next in the evolution of man. Fossils have been found all over the world and scientists can determine from these that he had an even larger brain, which enabled him to reason, speak, make plans and control how he moved his body. He is believed to have been a socialised being that used various weapons and tools.

Homo sapiens neanderthalensis were the next evolution of man, leading to our species today. This species appeared at the very end of the ice age and they were able to survive in very cold weather, because of their body size, which retained more body heat. They had even more social skills than the species before them, as well as a very strong and muscular build. The evolution of man was a long process, over approximately 5 million years, which resulted in the humans that reside on Earth today.

Q3a. Homo erectus evolved prior to Homo habilis.

Answer - B (FALSE)

The passage confirms that Homo erectus came after Homo habilis. The statement is false.

Q3b. Homo sapiens were capable of controlling their own body movement.

Answer - A (TRUE)

The information in the passage confirms that Homo sapiens were capable of controlling how the body moved. The statement is true.

Q3c. The human race is more than 5 million years old.

Answer - C (CANNOT SAY)

The passage states that scientists believe that human beings evolved from Order Primates. It goes on to state that Order Primates include chimpanzees, monkeys, gorillas and lemurs. It then moves on to disclose that scientists have gathered their information by studying fossils with the oldest dating back to more than 5 million years old.

Because the passage states that scientists believe the human race evolved from Order Primates, there is nothing to confirm in the passage that their belief is fact. Therefore, we cannot say if the statement is true or false based on the information provided.

Q3d. Homo habilis was able to speak.

Answer - C (CANNOT SAY)

The passage states that Homo habilis may have been able to speak. We cannot say whether this claim is true or false based on the information in the passage.

Q3e. Homo erectus was capable of eating meat.

Answer - A (TRUE)

The passage states that Homo erectus grew stronger and taller because of meat. The statement is true.

THE DIFFERENCE BETWEEN AFFECT AND EFFECT

Not everyone is skilled with grammar and even those who are struggle with some of the most commonly mistaken words in the English language. Two words that cause a lot of confusion for people are affect and effect. Many people have a lot of trouble with the usage and the meanings of these words, as they are very easy to mix up. The majority of people aren't really sure of when to use one or the other, which is why they simply end up guessing.

The reason why these two words are so confusing is that while each is a different part of speech, they sometimes function as other parts of speech.

[a]: In most cases, affect is a verb and effect is a noun. [b]: You can affect something, which will produce an effect on that thing. Things are always affected, never effected. This is the general rule that you should always remember. Only in rare cases will affect or effect serve as different parts of speech. [d]: Remember that an effect is always something that is produced and an affect is what you do to something.

Just to be thoroughly confusing, there are very rare situations when effect will be used as a verb and affect will be used as a noun. For the most part, you will never have to use them in these cases. Use the general rule from above (affect is a verb and effect is a noun), but try to remember the following odd instances. As a verb, effect means to accomplish, produce or execute something. As a noun, affect is used by psychologists to refer to desires and emotions as factors in how someone acts or thinks. Obviously, both of these instances do not occur often, but you will see them sometimes in things you may be reading, such as an academic journal. Always keep in your mind that under most circumstances, 'affect' is a verb and 'effect' is a noun.

Q4a. In most cases, 'effect' is a verb and 'affect' is a noun.

Answer - B (FALSE)

The passage states "In most cases, affect is a verb and effect is a noun". Did you notice that affect and effect had been swapped around in the statement? Therefore, the statement is false.

Q4b. If something is affected there will be a resultant effect on it.

Answer - A (TRUE)

The passage states that "You can affect something, which will produce an effect on that thing". The statement is true.

Q4c. There are occasions when effect will be used as a verb and affect will be used as a noun.

Answer - A (TRUE)

"Just to be thoroughly confusing, there are very rare situations when effect will be used as a verb and affect will be used as a noun." The statement is true.

Q4d. Affect can be described as what you do to something.

Answer - A (TRUE)

The passage confirms that affect is what you do to something. The statement is true.

Q4e. Affect is always something that is produced and an effect is what you do to something.

Answer - B (FALSE)

The passage states that "effect is always something that is produced and an affect is what you do to something". The statement is false.

MOUNT EVEREST

[a]: <u>Mount Everest is one of the most famous natural landmarks in the world; it is the highest point above sea level on Earth.</u> Many mountain climbers seek to climb Mount Everest as their ultimate goal and people visit in droves every single year to test their climbing skills on this peak. Here are some facts about Mount Everest to help you understand more about the mountain and its history.

- Everest is about 29,000 feet above sea level.

- The mountain was actually named by British surveyors for George Everest. [e]: <u>He was a famous Surveyor general of India throughout the mid-nineteenth century.</u>

- Everest has been altered considerably by five major glaciers, which still continue to change how the mountain looks. Glaciers have been credited with turning the mountain into a massive pyramid with three large ridges and three faces. [a]: <u>The best time to climb Everest is at the beginning of May. This will ensure that the monsoon season is avoided.</u>

- In 1975, the largest expedition to climb Everest was completed. A group of 410 people from China scaled the mountain together.

- One of the biggest problems that people face when climbing Everest is the extreme climate. The temperatures on the mountain never get above freezing and in the dead of winter they are well within negative temperatures. Climbers have to prepare not only for the lack of oxygen at altitude, but also for the incredibly cold temperatures.

- [b]: <u>Everest is rising ⅓ of an inch every single year. It is also very slowly moving northeastward, at about 3 inches per year.</u>

- Climbers Peter Habeler and Reinhold Messner have the distinction of being the first people to climb the mountain without supplemental oxygen. They did this in 1978.

- The safest year for climbers on Mount Everest was 1993. This is because 129 climbers made it all the way to the summit, with 8 deaths.

- 1996 is considered the least safe year on the mountain. 98 climbers made it to the summit, yet 15 died.

- The mountain is considered very sacred by those in Tibet and Nepal.

- [c]: <u>In Tibet, Mount Everest is called Chomolangma, which means 'goddess Mother of Snows', in the Tibetan language.</u> Those in Nepal refer to the mountain as Sagarmatha, which means 'Mother of the Universe'.

Q5a. The monsoon season starts after the month of May.

Answer - C (CANNOT SAY)

The passage states that by climbing Everest at the beginning of May you will avoid the monsoon season. We cannot tell from this information if the monsoon season is before the month of May or after it. Therefore, the correct answer is cannot say.

Q5b. Everest is increasing in height each year.

Answer - C (CANNOT SAY)

The passage states that Everest is rising by ⅓ of an inch per year. However, this does not mean that it is explicitly increasing in height. For example, 'rising' could mean that it could be rising above sea level, and not that it is actually increasing in height.

Q5c. To some people in Nepal, Mount Everest is also called Chomolangma, which means 'Goddess Mother of Snows'.

Answer - B (FALSE)

The passage states "In Tibet, Mount Everest is called Chomolangma, which means 'Goddess Mother of Snows', in the Tibetan language. The statement is false as it mentions people in Nepal, as opposed to Tibet.

Q5d. Everest is the tallest mountain in the world.

Answer - C (CANNOT SAY)

The passage states that Mount Everest is the highest point above sea level on Earth; therefore, it would be prudent to assume that it is the tallest mountain in the world. However, our task is not to assume and the correct answer is cannot say from the information provided. For example, there could be a mountain which is technically taller than Everest, but might start below sea level. Therefore, it would be the tallest mountain, but not the highest point above sea level.

Q5e. George Everest worked in India during the mid-nineteenth century.

Answer - A (TRUE)

The passage states that George Everest was a a surveyor general in India. Therefore, he worked in India.

THE CAMINO DE SANTIAGO

The Camino de Santiago was a major Christian pilgrimage route to the Cathedral of Santiago de Compostela in northwestern Spain. It dates back to medieval times and is still in existence today. This historic pilgrimage route has many interesting and unique things about it. Here are some facts and figures related to the Camino de Santiago:

- In English, The Camino de Santiago means 'The Way of Saint James', which is how many in the English-speaking world refer to this historic route.
- The Camino has been a Christian route for more than 1,000 years and many believe that it was used for other purposes long before that.
- The Camino was named as the very first European Cultural Route in 1987 by the Council of Europe. It is also one of UNESCO's world Heritage Sites.
- The symbol of the Camino de Santiago is the scallop shell. There are differing stories as to why, but many believe it is because the shell has multiple grooves that come together at a single point. This is a metaphor for how people came down many paths to end up at the Camino de Santiago.
- [e]: The earliest records of visitors to the Cathedral date back all
- the way to the 8th century.
- [d]: Pilgrims who travelled the route purchased a "credencial", or pilgrim's passport, from the Spanish government so that they could safely travel the route. They could show their passport at various pilgrim's hostels along the way in Spain and France, where they could stay overnight.
- [a]: Pilgrims who completed the walk along the Camino de Santiago were given a certificate of accomplishment called the Compostela. [c]: They had to walk at least 100 km in order to achieve this, but it was a very big honour for the devout people that had travelled to the Cathedral.
- Every day at noon, a pilgrim's mass is held at the Cathedral of Santiago de Compostela in honour of the pilgrims.
- On special Holy Years, more pilgrims than ever take the route. The last Holy Year was 2010, when more than 272,000 pilgrims walked the route to the Cathedral.
- [b]: The next Holy Year is in 2021. Holy Years are when the sacred holiday of Saint James's Day (July 25), falls on a Sunday.

Q6a. The people who walk the Camino de Santiago are known as pilgrims.

Answer - A (TRUE)

The passage confirms that "Pilgrims who completed the walk along the Camino de Santiago were given a certificate of accomplishment called the Compostela". The answer is true.

Q6b. The next Holy Year will be 2012.

Answer - B (FALSE)

The passage states the next Holy Year will be 2021. The statement is false.

Q6c. The Camino de Santiago is 100 km long.

Answer - C (CANNOT SAY)

The passage only makes reference to the fact that pilgrims had to walk at least 100km of the Camino de Santiago in order to receive their certificate of accomplishment. It makes no reference to how long the route is; therefore, the correct answer is cannot say based on the information provided.

Q6d. A credencial is a pilgrim's passport that enables them to travel safely.

Answer - A (TRUE)

According to the passage, this statement is true.

Q6e. People have been walking the Camino de Santiago since the 8th century.

Answer - C (CANNOT SAY)

The passage states that "The earliest records of visitors to the Cathedral date back all the way to the 8th century". This only confirms that visitors to the Cathedral date back to the 8th century and not actual walkers of the route. Therefore, we cannot say based on the information provided.

THE EUROPEAN UNION

The European Union was officially established in 1993 under its current name. The history of the EU and its current actions are something that many people are not fully aware of. Here are some interesting facts and figures about the European Union.

- The Maastricht Treaty of 1993 formally named the European Union.
- The EU traces its roots all the way back to the European Coal and Steel Community and the European Economic Community, formed together by six member countries in 1958.
- [c]: The Eu has a combined population of 500 million inhabitants in 27 member states. This is 7.3% of the world's population.
- The eurozone, which is a monetary union within the European Union, was established in 1999. 5: There are 17 member states (countries) in the eurozone, all of which utilise the euro as their form of currency. This enables free spending in all of the eurozone countries without having to exchange currencies, making movement from country to country much easier.
- There are many important institutions of the EU, such as the European Commission, Council of the European Union, the European Council, the European Central Bank, and the Court Justice of the European Union.
- European Parliament is part of the legislative function of the EU and members are directly elected from each member country every 5 years.
- The anthem of the European Union is "Ode to Joy".
- In the entire organisation there are 23 different languages spoken.
- [a]: The euro currency was introduced on January 1, 2002, where it was printed and distributed throughout 12 member countries. This was a huge logistical operation, with nearly 80 billion coins involved.
- 38,000 people are employed by the European Commission.
- 1% of the annual budget of the EU is spent on staff and administra- tion, as well as continued maintenance on buildings.
- The European Commission is hailed as having one of the largest translation centres in the world, with 1,750 linguists. There are also 600 support staff members for the linguists.
- European Parliament holds its regular committee meetings in Brussels.
- [b]: The Eu has the world's third largest population, after China and India.
- The EU's GDP is now bigger than that of the US.

Q7a. There are currently 12 countries using the Euro currency.

Answer - B (FALSE)

The passage states that there are 17 member states using the Euro as currency. Therefore, there are more than 12 countries using the Euro. The statement is false.

Q7b. There are more people living in the European Union than China.

Answer - B (FALSE)

The passage confirms that "The EU has the world's third largest population, after China and India". The answer is false as there are more people living in China than the European Union.

Q7c. 7.3% of the world's population live in the European Union.

Answer - A (TRUE)

According to the passage, this statement is true.

Q7d. Greece is in the European Union.

Answer - C (CANNOT SAY)

The passage makes no mention of Greece being in the European Union. Therefore, we cannot say based on the information provided.

Q7e. One of the benefits of the eurozone is that it negates the need to change currency between the different countries that form part of it.

Answer - A (TRUE)

The passage states "There are 17 member states in the eurozone, all of which utilise the euro as their form of currency. This enables free spending in all of the eurozone countries without having to exchange currencies, making movement from country to country much easier". The passage confirms that the statement is true.

RULES OF AMERICAN FOOTBALL

American football is an incredibly popular sport all over the United States, but it is less popular throughout other countries. An increasing number of people in the UK are starting to play and watch this classic American sport. If you want to be able to play, or understand the sport while watching it on television, you need to know the rules. Here is an overview of the basic rules of American football.

OFFENSE AND DEFENSE

Each team has 11 players on the field at one time. The team that has pos- session of the football is the offense, and their objective is to advance the ball down the field. They do this by running with the ball, or passing it to another team-mate. They score points when they get to the very end of the field, crossing the goal line into the end zone. The team that does not have the ball is the defense. Their objective is to prevent the other team from getting into the end zone and scoring a touchdown. They do this by attempting to block players from catching passes, tackling players who are running with the ball, and/or trying to catch passes that are intended for the offensive team (catching such a pass is called an interception).

[b]: If the offensive team scores, or if they lose possession of the ball to the defense, then the two teams switch roles. This continues on until the four timed quarters of the game have been completed. [c]:The game is divided into four 15-minute quarters, along with a half-time break of 12 minutes. The teams change ends of the field after each quarter.

THE FIELD

[e]: A football field measures 100 yards long and is 53 yards wide. There are markers on the field to tell the players, coaches and officials which yard line they are on. Every 10 yards is marked by a line. The end zone is also marked and is at the 0-yard line on the field. This zone is 10 yards long, but does not count towards the 100 yards of the field.

SCORING

[a & e]: If the offense makes it to the end zone, they score a touchdown, which is six points. They can then either kick a field goal for an extra point, or they can do a small play in the last 10 yards of the field which is called a two-point conversion and is worth two points. If they do not score a touchdown and decide to try for a field goal, they can score three points. There are many other intricate rules of American football, but the above are all of the most important aspects.

Q8a. In American Football you can only score points when the ball crosses the goal line into the end zone via a touchdown.

Answer - B (FALSE)

The statement is false as there are alternative ways to score points other than a touchdown in the end zone.

Q8b. When a team does not have the ball they are the defense.

Answer - A (TRUE)

The passage states that "If the offensive team scores, or if they lose possession of the ball to the defense, then the two teams switch roles." Therefore, the statement is true.

Q8c. The game of American Football, excluding breaks, is 60 minutes in duration.

Answer - A (TRUE)

The passage states "The game is divided into four 15-minute quarters, along with a half-time break of 12 minutes. The teams change ends of the field after each quarter." Therefore, the total duration of the game, excluding breaks, is 60 minutes. The statement is true.

Q8d. The protective helmets worn by American Footballers are designed to protect the head from injury.

Answer - C (CANNOT SAY)

The passage makes no reference to the helmets that are worn by the players, or their intended purpose. The correct answer is cannot say based on the information provided.

Q8e. A football field measures 100 yards wide and 53 yards long.

Answer - B (FALSE)

The passage states that the length is 100 yards and the width is 53 yards. The answer is false.

FACTS ABOUT THE NATIONAL GEOGRAPHIC

[b]: The National Geographic Society (NGS) is a group that is headquartered in Washington, DC in the United States, which publishes a magazine titled National Geographic. The group and the fascinating magazine it releases are very interesting to many people all over the world, as they have made huge strides in environmental and historical preservation, among other things.

- [d]: The National Geographic Society was founded on January 27, 1888 by Gardiner Greene Hubbard.

- [c]: Worldwide membership of the society is currently at about 8.5 million people.

- The logo for the NGS is a rectangular yellow portrait frame, which can be found as its television logo and on the margins surrounding the front cover of their magazine.

- [e]: The organisation is designed to fund research and preservation of historical, archaeological, and natural science areas throughout the entire world. It is a non-profit organisation.

- The Society has given grants for scientific research since it began, and recently gave out its 10,000th grant.

- The NGS began as a group for elite world travellers and academics that were wealthy and interested in advancing tourism and interest in history, science and culture.

- In 2004, the NGS headquarters in washington, DC was one of the first buildings ever to receive a Green Certification from Global Green USA.

- The magazine started nine months after the society was founded in October 1888. It is published 12 times per year, along with at least four supplements.

- [a]: More than 50 million readers all over the world read National Geographic every month, in 32 different languages.

- NGS has funded more than 9,600 conservation, research and exploration projects throughout the entire Earth.

- In addition to the magazine, NGS reaches more than 400 million people per month through videos, their television channel, books, radio, music, films, interactive media and more.

Q9a. More than 50 million readers all over the world read National Geographic every year, in 32 different languages.

Answer - A (TRUE)

The passage states that "More than 50 million readers all over the world read National Geographic every month, in 32 different languages". The statement, however, is slightly different as it states every year. If there are more than 50 million readers every month then there are more than 50 million readers every year. The statement is true.

Q9b. The National Geographic Society's magazine is not titled National Geographic.

Answer - B (FALSE)

According to the passage this statement is false. The magazine is titled National Geographic.

Q9c. The National Geographic Society has 50 million members all over the world in 32 different languages.

Answer - B (FALSE)

The statement is false. The passage confirms that the "worldwide membership of the society is currently at about 8.5 million people."

Q9d. The National Geographic Society was founded over 100 years ago.

Answer - A (TRUE)

The passage states "The National Geographic Society was founded on January 27, 1888 by Gardiner Greene Hubbard". Therefore, the statement is true as the society was founded over 100 years ago.

Q9e. The National Geographic Society is a profitable business.

Answer - B (FALSE)

The passage states that the National Geographic is a non-profit organisation. The statement is false.

INTERNAL COMBUSTION ENGINE THEORY

Internal combustion engines are the most commonly used engines in the entire world. They are used in a wide range of vehicles and chances are if you drive a car, yours uses this type of engine. [e]: They are also used in industrial applications and largely replaced the steam engine throughout the 20th century.

WHAT IS THE THEORY?

The main principle behind any type of internal combustion engine is if you put a small amount of a type of high-energy fuel, such as gasoline, into a very small space and ignite it, a large amount of energy will be released in the form of gas that expands. This energy can then be used to propel almost anything and it is very effective. [a]: This is why the majority of common vehicle engines are built based upon this theory. This prin- ciple is the core that most car engines today are built on.

HOW IT WORKS

The engine utilises a fossil fuel inside of a combustion chamber and com- bines this with an oxidiser, which is usually air. [d]: When the air and the fossil fuel are heated in the combustion chamber, the gas and the air will expand. The expansion of the gas and the air when combustion is applied causes a force to the pistons, turbine blades, or nozzle inside of the engine. This then transforms the chemical energy of the internal combustion energy into mechanical energy that powers the vehicle or industrial application.

Most cars on the roads right now use a four-stroke combustion cycle. This converts gasoline so that it can propel the car forward. This is also called the 'Otto Cycle', as it is named after the inventor, Nikolaus Otto, who invented it in 1867. These four strokes are called the intake stroke, compression stroke, combustion stroke, and the exhaust stroke.

[b]: The first internal combustion engine was created by Jean Joseph Étienne lenoir, a Belgian engineer, in 1859. [c]: Without his application of the theory, we might not have the advanced vehicle engines we have today.

Q10a. The majority of vehicle engines are built based upon the internal combustion engine theory.

Answer - A (TRUE)

The passage confirms this statement to be true.

Q10b. The first internal combustion engine was built in Belgium.

Answer - C (CANNOT SAY)

The passage states "The first internal combustion engine was created by Jean Joseph Étienne Lenoir, a Belgian engineer, in 1859". Although the passage indicates that the creator of the first internal combustion engine was a Belgian engineer, this does not confirm that the first engine was actually built in Belgium. Therefore, we cannot say without further information whether the statement is true or false.

Q10c. Without the internal combustion engine we would not have the motor vehicle.

Answer - C (CANNOT SAY)

The passage states "Without his application of the theory, we might not have the advanced vehicle engines we have today". There is a difference between 'might not have' and 'would not have'. The correct answer is 'cannot say'.

Q10d. Gas and air expansion in the combustion chamber occurs when air and fossil fuel are heated.

Answer - A (TRUE)

The statement is true because the passage states "When the air and the fossil fuel are heated in the combustion chamber, the gas and the air will expand".

Q10e. Internal combustion engines replaced the steam engine in the 20th century.

Answer - B (FALSE)

The passage states "They are also used in industrial applications and largely replaced the steam engine throughout the 20th century". Whilst they largely replaced steam engines the passage does not say they replaced them entirely. The statement is false.

HOW A FRIDGE WORKS

Refrigerators are widely popular everywhere in the world and they are a vital part of any kitchen. If you want to be able to keep food fresh and chilled to the correct temperature, you will need one of these appliances. Not only are they useful, there are also attractive and innovative models that add to the aesthetic appeal of your kitchen. You probably see your fridge multiple times per day but are unaware how it works.

PARTS OF A FRIDGE

To understand how a fridge works, first you have to know what parts are inside of it. [c]: Every refrigerator has five main components that help it to keep your food and drinks cold.

THE COOLING PROCESS

When you turn on your fridge, it does not automatically become cold. There are intricate processes at work inside of the appliance. [e]: The first thing that happens when your fridge is turned on is that the refrigerant liquid, which is contained within the coils, is compressed into a gas by the compressor. The gas will heat up as it becomes pressurised. [a]: The exterior heat-exchange pipes that reside on the rear panel of the unit then lose heat as the hot refrigerant gas dissipates it. The gas will then condense into liquid when it is under this high pressure. This pressurised refrigerant liquid will flow through the expansion valve, which is essentially a very tiny hole. One side of the hole will have the high-pressure liquid, while the other side will have the low-pressure gas that the compressor is pulling from.

[d]: Once the liquid flows through the expansion valve, which is essential to the running of the fridge, it will start to boil and turn into a vapour, which drops its temperature. This will cool down the refrigerator. The cold refrigerant gas will then go back through the compressor and the entire process will be repeated.

Q11a. Exterior heat-exchanging pipes are located externally on the rear panel.

Answer - A (TRUE)

The passage states "The exterior heat-exchange pipes that reside on the rear panel of the unit then lose heat as the hot refrigerant gas dissipates it". The statement is true based on this information.

Q11b. Fridges are commonly known as 'white goods'.

Answer - C (CANNOT SAY)

Although this statement is true in everyday life, the passage makes no reference to it. We cannot say based on the information provided.

Q11c. In total there are five components to the fridge.

Answer - C (CANNOT SAY)

Although the passage states that there are 5 main components, it does not confirm that these are the total number of components. The answer is 'cannot say'.

Q11d. Without the expansion valve the fridge will not operate correctly.

Answer - A (TRUE)

The passage confirms that the expansion valve is essential to the running of the fridge; therefore, the statement is true.

Q11e. The refrigerant liquid becomes a gas.

Answer - A (TRUE)

"The first thing that happens when your fridge is turned on is that the refrigerant liquid, which is contained within the coils, is compressed into a gas by the compressor." The statement is true based on the information provided in the passage.

HOW AN AEROPLANES FLIES

There are three principles that you have to understand in order to fully grasp how an aeroplane is able to fly and how it does this effectively. Getting to know The Bernouilli Effect, The Coanda Effect and Newton's Third Law will help you to understand how an aeroplane flies.

THE BERNOUILLI EFFECT

The Bernouilli Effect explains how the wings enable the aeroplane to fly.

[d]: <u>The wings are curved into a specific shape to make what is called an airfoil.</u> On the majority of aircrafts, the bottom of the wing (or airfoil) is flat, while the top is a more curved surface. [c]: <u>Air will flow very fast over the top because of the shape, which thins this air considerably. This thinner air at the top of the airfoil creates a strong vacuum, which pulls up on the wing.</u> This is how the lifting action is generated and this keeps the aeroplane in the sky.

THE COANDA EFFECT

The Coanda Effect is another force that helps to keep the plane in the air. This is a principle of physics that says that a jet of fluid will most often tend to follow along a curved surface. This is another important factor in keeping the curved wings and body of the plane in the air.

NEWTON'S THIRD LAW

Newton's Third Law explains another reason why an aeroplane will fly. The trailing edge of the wing curves in a downward fashion, so that when air flows over this, it will angle in a downward motion off the wing and shoot out fast behind it. Newton's Third Law of thermodynamics is a principle in physics. It explains that for any action that occurs, there is an opposite and equal reaction to it. As the wing pushes downward and forces are behind it, the air will push the wing upwards. [e]: <u>This principle, along with The Bernouilli Effect, explains how an aeroplane will stay in the air.</u> Essentially, it is because of the advanced design of the wings and the body of the plane.

Q12a. Millions of people fly on aeroplanes each year.

Answer - C (CANNOT SAY)

There is nothing in the passage to confirm this statement. The correct answer is 'cannot say'.

Q12b. Newton's Third Law is named so because it is the third law in the process of flight.

Answer - C (CANNOT SAY)

Once again, there is nothing in the passage to confirm this statement. Just because the law is listed third in the passage sequence does not mean the law is the third one in the process of flight. The correct answer is 'cannot say'.

Q12c. The air flow over the top of a wing is faster than the air flow underneath the wing.

Answer - C (CANNOT SAY)

The passage does confirm that air will flow very fast over the top. However, it does not confirm that air flowing over the top of the wing is faster that the flow underneath the wing. The correct answer is 'cannot say'.

Q12d. The wings on an aeroplane are curved so that the air can flow faster over them.

Answer - A (TRUE)

The passage states "The wings are curved into a specific shape to make what is called an airfoil. On the majority of aircrafts, the bottom of the wing (or airfoil) is flat, while the top is a more curved surface".

The passage then goes on to state "Air will flow very fast over the top because of the shape, which thins this air considerably".

From the information in the two paragraphs above the statement is true.

Q12e. The body of a plane has nothing to do with the aeroplane staying in the air.

Answer - B (FALSE)

The passage states "This principle, along with The Bernouilli Effect, explains how an aeroplane will stay in the air. Essentially, it is because of the advanced design of the wings and the body of the plane".

The statement is false because the body of the plane does have something to do with the aeroplane staying in the air.

500 MORE VERBAL REASONING QUESTIONS

In this chapter, you wil find an extra 500 Verbal Reasoning questions, ranging across 20 different question types. These questions cover the following areas:

- Insert the letter;
- Odd ones out (two);
- Four-letter code;
- Closest in meaning;
- Hidden word in the sentence;
- Three missing letters;
- Letters for numbers code;
- Move the letter;
- Letter sequences;
- Word relations;
- Find the compound word;
- Word fusion;
- Connecting letters;
- Opposite meanings (one from each group);
- Completing the sum;
- Number relations;
- Number/word codes;
- Completing the word.

Take your time answering these questions, and make sure to read the answers and explanations once you've finished each section.

These question types appear in a range of different Verbal Reasoning exams. So, while you might not face all of them, it's likely that you'll have to complete at least one or two in a verbal reasoning assessment.

We recommend that you give yourself 25 minutes for each section. However, if you do get stuck, try answering them at your own pace so that you can nail the method for each question type. Good luck!

Question Type 1 - Insert the Letter

Find the letter that completes each word. This letter will finish the first word, and start the second word in each set. The letter must be the same in both sets.

Example:

Bal (?) ack   Tal (?) ake

	L	D	M	E

Answer = Ball Lack   Tall Lake

Explanation = 'L' creates 'Ball', 'Lack', 'Tall', and 'Lake'.

Question 1

Bal (?) int   Cal (?) ild

	M	D	T	K

Question 2

Wor (?) ale   Wal (?) nit

	N	K	B	T

Question 3

Bul (?) ook   Tom (?) ull

	T	E	B	N

Question 4

Tol (?) olt   Hol (?) oor

	D	H	N	U

Question 5

Bur (?) orm   Tur (?) ile

T   N   B   U

Question 6

Bol (?) art   Hol (?) eal

I   N   B   D

Question 7

Bar (?) arn   Har (?) ach

N   E   F   T

Question 8

Hoo (?) ulp   Gul (?) ond

D   P   T   A

Question 9

Mel (?) ire   Fol (?) irt

T   D   E   Y

Question 10

Gur (?) gly   Men (?) ndo

Y   R   U   B

Question 11

Mak (?) ars   Mar (?) nvy

B   E   I   R

Question 12

Bee (?) ear   Cur (?) old

T   D   Y   N

Question 13

Ren (?) eal   Gol (?) ial

E   D   H   A

Question 14

Bac (?) ick   Bar (?) iss

E   P   K   T

Question 15

Hal (?) ome   Sal (?) rip

P   D   E   T

Question 16

Ope (?) ick   Ano (?) erd

M   N   E   O

Question 17

Doo (?) old   Loo (?) elt

N   D   M   T

Question 18

Fis (?) ilt   Mal (?) all

T   K   E   B

Question 19

Sol (?) pal   Pol (?) Ast

A   T   O   L

Question 20

Soa (?) ull   Bur (?) oll

R   Y   B   P

Question 21

Pal (?) pic   Lat (?) rgo

T   E   L   O

Question 22

Tic (?) ill   Amo (?) ook

T   K   A   D

Question 23

	Cod (?) Xis	Ide (?) Xel	
A	E	U	T

Question 24

	Afa (?) aid	Gea (?) uin	
T	C	L	R

Question 25

	Vie (?) ool	Avo (?) alk	
L	W	C	E

Answers to Question Type 1

Question 1

Answer = M

Explanation = Balm and Mint, Calm and Mild

Question 2

Answer = K

Explanation = Work and Kale, Walk and Knit

Question 3

Answer = B

Explanation = Bulb and Book, Tomb and Bull

Question 4

Answer = D

Explanation = Told and Dolt, Hold and Door

Question 5

Answer = N

Explanation = Burn and Norm, Turn and Nile

Question 6

Answer = D

Explanation = Bold and Dart, Hold and Deal

Question 7

Answer = E

Explanation = Bare and Earn, Hare and Each

Question 8

Answer = P

Explanation = Hoop and Pulp, Gulp and Pond

Question 9

Answer = D

Explanation = Meld and Dire, Fold and Dirt

Question 10

Answer = U

Explanation = Guru and Ugly, Menu and Undo

Question 11

Answer = E

Explanation = Make and Ears, Mare and Envy

Question 12

Answer = T

Explanation = Beet and Tear, Curt and Told

Question 13

Answer = D

Explanation = Rend and Deal, Gold and Dial

Question 14

Answer = K

Explanation = Back and Kick, Bark and Kiss

Question 15

Answer = T

Explanation = Halt and Tome, Salt and Trip

Question 16

Answer = N

Explanation = Open and Nick, Anon and Nerd

Question 17

Answer = M

Explanation = Doom and Mold, Loom and Melt

Question 18

Answer = T

Explanation = Fist and Tilt, Malt and Tall

Question 19

Answer = O

Explanation = Solo and Opal, Polo and Oast

Question 20

Answer = P

Explanation = Soap and Pull, Burp and Poll

Question 21

Answer = E

Explanation = Pale and Epic, Late and Ergo

Question 22

Answer = K

Explanation = Tick and Kill, Amok and Kook

Question 23

Answer = A

Explanation = Coda and Axis, Idea and Axel

Question 24

Answer = R

Explanation = Afar and Raid, Gear and Ruin

Question 25

Answer = W

Explanation = View and Wool, Avow and Walk

Question Type 2 - Odd Ones Out

In each question, there are five words. Three of these words are related, and two are not. Find the two words which are not related to the other three.

Example:

A	B	C	D	E
Tiger	Lion	Dog	Fox	Leopard

Answer = C and D.

Explanation = Tigers, lions, and leopards are all 'big cats'. Dogs and foxes are not.

Question 1

A	B	C	D	E
Divide	Fraction	Multiply	Add	Decimal

Question 2

A	B	C	D	E
Rubber	Leather	Concrete	Fur	Silk

Question 3

A	B	C	D	E
Air	Wet	Fire	Hot	Earth

Question 4

A	B	C	D	E
Pitch	Age	Volume	Timbre	Function

Question 5

A	B	C	D	E
Form	Structure	Interpret	Content	Consider

Question 6

A	B	C	D	E
Stapler	Pen	Crayon	Pencil	Eraser

Question 7

A	B	C	D	E
Poker	Chess	Roulette	Blackjack	Draughts

Question 8

A	B	C	D	E
Tombstone	Waiting Room	Mausoleum	Morgue	Tunnel

Question 9

A	B	C	D	E
City	King	Town	Emperor	Kingdom

Question 10

A	B	C	D	E
Sun	Venus	Moon	Mars	Neptune

Question 11

A	B	C	D	E
Circle	Trapezium	Cube	Oval	Cylinder

Question 12

A	B	C	D	E
Red	Easel	Green	Orange	Brush

Question 13

A	B	C	D	E
Knife	Skewer	Rolling Pin	Chopping Board	Cleaver

Question 14

A	B	C	D	E
Soil	Sand	Compost	Mould	Stone

Question 15

A	B	C	D	E
Hunt	Hunter	Prey	Chase	Capture

Question 16

A	B	C	D	E
Dog	Cat	Cheetah	Hamster	Elephant

Question 17

A	B	C	D	E
Physics	English	History	Biology	Psychology

Question 18

A	B	C	D	E
England	Lancashire	Scotland	Wales	Kent

Question 19

A	B	C	D	E
Instruct	Conflict	War	Resolve	Fight

Question 20

A	B	C	D	E
Child	Grow	Adult	Pensioner	Frail

Question 21

A	B	C	D	E
Denim	Cotton	Canvas	Aluminium	Cardboard

Question 22

A	B	C	D	E
Slab	Door	Rock	Boulder	Staircase

Question 23

A	B	C	D	E
Collar	Cuff	Cut	Sleeve	Roll

Question 24

A	B	C	D	E
Thermometer	Thermostat	Degrees	Fahrenheit	Mercury

Question 25

A	B	C	D	E
Operating System	Keyboard	Mouse	Word Processor	Monitor

Answers to Question Type 2

Question 1

Answer = B and E

Explanation = Divide, Multiply, and Add are all verb forms for mathematical operations. Fractions and Decimals are nouns, and are not operations.

Question 2

Answer = A and C

Explanation = Leather, fur, and silk are all sourced from animals. Rubber and concrete are not.

Question 3

Answer = B and D

Explanation = Wet and Hot are both adjectives used to describe nouns like Air, Fire, and Earth.

Question 4

Answer = B and E

Explanation = Pitch, Volume, and Timbre are all concepts used to describe sound and musical noises. Age and Function are not.

Question 5

Answer = C and E

Explanation = Interpret and Consider are both verbs. Form, Structure, and Content are all nouns associated with literary theory.

Question 6

Answer = A and E

Explanation = While these are all stationery objects, pen, crayon, and pencil are used to write or draw on paper or another surface. Staplers and erasers do not perform this function.

Question 7

Answer = B and E

Explanation = Poker, Roulette, and Blackjack are all activities associated with gambling or wagers. Chess and Draughts are not.

Question 8

Answer = B and E

Explanation = Tombstone, Mausoleum, and Morgue are all terms associated with death. Waiting room and tunnel are not.

Question 9

Answer = B and D

Explanation = City, Town, and Kingdom are all words for areas of land. King and Emperor are positions of power.

Question 10

Answer = A and C

Explanation = Venus, Mars, and Neptune are all names of planets. Sun and Moon are not.

Question 11

Answer = C and E

Explanation = Circle, Trapezium, and Oval are all two-dimensional shapes. Cube and Cylinder are three-dimensional shapes.

Question 12

Answer = B and E

Explanation = Red, Green, and Orange are all colours. Easel and Brush are tools used in painting.

Question 13

Answer = C and D

Explanation = All of these objects are involved in the preparation of food. However, only Knife, Skewer, and Cleaver are sharp objects.

Question 14

Answer = D and E

Explanation = Soil, Sand, and Compost are grainy substances found in the earth. Mould and Stone are not.

Question 15

Answer = B and C

Explanation = While all of these words are associated with hunting, Hunt, Chase, and Capture are verbs. Hunter and Prey are both nouns.

Question 16

Answer = C and E

Explanation = Dog, Cat, and Hamster are domesticated animals. Cheetah and Elephant are not.

Question 17

Answer = B and C

Explanation = Physics, Biology, and Psychology are sciences. English and History are not.

Question 18

Answer = B and E

Explanation = England, Scotland, and Wales are all countries in the United Kingdom. Lancashire and Kent are counties.

Question 19

Answer = A and D

Explanation = Conflict, War, and Fight are all terms associated with violence.

Question 20

Answer = B and E

Explanation = Child, Adult, and Pensioner are all nouns associated with age. Grow is a verb, and Frail is an adjective.

Question 21

Answer = D and E

Explanation = Denim, Cotton, and Canvas are all materials associated with clothing. Aluminium and Cardboard are not.

Question 22

Answer = B and E

Explanation = Slab, Rock, and Boulder are all naturally-occurring pieces of stone. Door and Staircase are sculpted.

Question 23

Answer = C and E

Explanation = Collar, Cuff, and Sleeve are all part of a piece of clothing such as a shirt.

Question 24

Answer = C and D

Explanation = Degrees and Fahrenheit are both units of measurement, while Thermometer, Thermostat and Mercury are objects or substances associated with measuring temperature.

Question 25

Answer = A and D

Explanation = Keyboard, Mouse, and Monitor are all pieces of computer hardware (also known as peripherals). Operating System and Word Processor are both pieces of software or firmware.

Question Type 3 - Four-Letter Code

For each question, figure out the code. An alphabet is provided to help you.

A B C D E F G H I J K L M N O P Q R S T U V W X Y Z

Example:

If the code for MACE is OCEG, what does EQNF mean?

Answer = COLD

Question 1

If the code for REEL is TGGN, what does FKTV mean?

A	B	C	D
MELT	DIRT	BELT	HURT

Question 2

If the code for CORD is ZLOA, what does HFKD mean?

A	B	C	D
KIND	COIN	KING	KILN

Question 3

If the code for DRAIN is NBKSX, what does LKCUOD mean?

A	B	C	D
BASKET	BURIED	ATTACH	INSANE

Question 4

If the code for CONTROL is BHGJIHF, what does AHHIHABD mean?

A	B	C	D
COMPOSED	APPRAISE	APPROACH	INTRUDE

A B C D E F G H I J K L M N O P Q R S T U V W X Y Z

Question 5

If the code for ACCEPT is SODBBZ, what does XZQSDA mean?

A	B	C	D
ADVISE	ABSORB	BEHOLD	BETRAY

Question 6

If the code for DAMAGE is AWIWCA, what does ODWHHKS mean?

A	B	C	D
ALLOYS	SWALLOW	FOLLOW	SHALLOW

Question 7

If the code for INDICATOR is TYOTNLEZC, what does QZCRZEEPY mean?

A	B	C	D
FORGOTTEN	EXCITABLE	FABRICATE	FAINTNESS

Question 8

If the code for GRIP is FKGJ, what does CKECH mean?

A	B	C	D
IRATE	BREAK	BRAID	GRATE

Question 9

If the code for TIDE is WLGH, what does EXUGHQ mean?

A	B	C	D
BARROW	BRIBED	BURDEN	TOILET

A B C D E F G H I J K L M N O P Q R S T U V W X Y Z

Question 10

If the code for COURAGE is OQKBEYM, what does IBODCKW mean?

A	B	C	D
MASTERY	WITHOLD	ATROPHY	CONSUME

Question 11

If the code for BRAVE is DTCXG , what is the code for BEARD?

A	B	C	D
DGCTF	DFTCA	BFTGC	TPLOT

Question 12

If the code for CURATE is KCZIBM, what is the code for EMBOLDEN?

A	B	C	D
MGAUTSAG	TSUGATGP	OLAGNTTE	MUJWTLMV

Question 13

If the code for DOLLAR is HDBBBJ, what does FDBBJB mean?

A	B	C	D
GALLON	FALLEN	CALLER	POLLEN

Question 14

If the code for CHARACTER is EJCTCEVGT, then what does CFFTGUU mean?

A	B	C	D
CORRECT	ADDRESS	SUPPOSE	PROJECT

A B C D E F G H I J K L M N O P Q R S T U V W X Y Z

Question 15

If the code for UNBEARABLE is KDRUQHQRBU, what does QSSUFJQRBU mean?

A	B	C	D
ACCEPTABLE	ACCENTUATE	TASKMASTER	TEMPERANCE

Question 16

If the code for DRAGON is QRJDUG, what does QRLWLVRS mean?

A	B	C	D
AUDITION	AMBITION	POSITION	VOLITION

Question 17

If the code for SUMMER is YKPVGT, what is the code for SPRING?

A	B	C	D
CWVWOP	TVUVPT	URTKPI	GHQTVQ

Question 18

If the code for UNEARTH is PIZVMOC, what is the code for PROTEST?

A	B	C	D
SLOTSNT	KMJOZNO	TNAHGAT	DNOOLFA

Question 19

If the code for ATTRIBUTE is KDDBSLEDO, what does SXDBSQEO mean?

A	B	C	D
INTENDED	INTRIGUE	INTEGRAL	INTERNAL

A B C D E F G H I J K L M N O P Q R S T U V W X Y Z

Question 20

If the code for BALLOON is NLXXAAZ, what does MPYUF mean?

A	B	C	D
ADMIT	ERODE	AUDIT	BOARD

Question 21

If the code for ADULT is VNWFC, what does FYQTE mean?

A	B	C	D
BUILD	GROWN	CROWD	UNTIL

Question 22

If the code for TUTORING is IJIDGXCV, what is the code for DEPRIVE?

A	B	C	D
BRKTEGX	STEGXKT	LOGSTSG	PLFQFGN

Question 23

If the code for BURIAL is OHEVNY, what is the code for INTEND?

A	B	C	D
QRYTXV	OINTYN	PILNPD	VAGRAQ

Question 24

If the code for JESTER is OJXYJW, what does HTWWZUY mean?

A	B	C	D
HORRIFY	CORRUPT	BARRELS	JARRING

A B C D E F G H I J K L M N O P Q R S T U V W X Y Z

Question 25

If the code for JUPITER is BMHALWJ, what is the code for APOLLO?

A	B	C	D
SKDKKQ	OLOTTV	SHGDDG	AVLTOP

Answers to Question Type 3

Question 1

Answer = B – Dirt

Explanation = Each letter corresponds with a letter 2 spaces ahead of it. So, D becomes F, I becomes K, R becomes T, and T becomes V.

Question 2

Answer = C – King

Explanation = Each letter corresponds with a letter 3 spaces behind it. So, K becomes H, I becomes F, N becomes K, and G becomes D.

Question 3

Answer = A – Basket

Explanation = Each letter corresponds with a letter 10 spaces ahead of it. So, B becomes L, A becomes K, S becomes C, K becomes U, E becomes O, and T becomes D.

Question 4

Answer = C – Approach

Explanation = If each letter is assigned a value from 1 to 26 (A = 1, B = 2, etc), then each letter corresponds with a letter which is half of its value, rounded up to the nearest whole number. So, A is A, P is H, R is I, O is H, C is B, and H is D.

Question 5

Answer = D – Betray

Explanation = Each letter corresponds to the letter just before it. So, B becomes A, E becomes D, and so on to give ADSQZX. Then, the word is reversed. So, ADSQZX becomes XZQSDA.

Question 6

Answer = D - Shallow

Explanation = Each letter corresponds to the letter 4 spaces behind it. So, S becomes O, H becomes D, A becomes W, L becomes H, O becomes K, and W becomes S.

Question 7

Answer = A – Forgotten

Explanation = Each letter corresponds to the letter 11 spaces ahead of it. So, F becomes Q, O becomes Z, R becomes C, G becomes R, T becomes E, E becomes P, and N becomes Y.

Question 8

Answer = B – Break

Explanation = Each letter is assigned a value (A = 1, B = 2, and so on). The letter corresponds to a letter which is half of the value (rounded up to the nearest whole number), plus 2. So, B becomes C, R becomes K, E becomes E, A becomes C, and K becomes H.

Question 9

Answer = C – Burden

Explanation = Each letter corresponds to the letter 3 spaces ahead of it. So, B becomes E, U becomes X, R becomes U, D becomes G, E becomes H, and N becomes Q.

Question 10

Answer = A – Mastery

Explanation = Each letter corresponds to the letter 10 spaces ahead of it. So, M becomes W, A becomes K, S becomes C, T becomes D, E becomes O, R becomes B, and Y becomes I. Then, the word is reversed.

Question 11

Answer = A – DGCTF

Explanation = Each letter corresponds to the letter 2 spaces ahead of it. So, B becomes D, E becomes G, A becomes C, R becomes T, and D becomes F.

Question 12

Answer = D – MUJWTLMV

Explanation = Each letter corresponds with a letter 8 spaces ahead of it. So, E becomes M, M becomes U, B becomes J, O becomes W, L becomes T, D becomes L, and N becomes V.

Question 13

Answer = D – POLLEN

Explanation = Each letter is assigned a value (A = 1, B = 2, and so on). Each letter corresponds to a letter which is double its value. So, P becomes F, O becomes D, L becomes B, E becomes J, and N becomes B.

Question 14

Answer = B – ADDRESS

Explanation = Each letter corresponds with the letter 2 spaces ahead of it. So, A becomes C, D becomes F, R becomes T, E becomes G, and S becomes U.

Question 15

Answer = A – ACCEPTABLE

Explanation = Each letter corresponds with the letter 10 spaces behind it. So, A becomes Q, C becomes S, E becomes U, P becomes F, T becomes J, B becomes R, and L becomes B.

Question 16

Answer = C – POSITION

Explanation = Each letter corresponds with the letter 3 spaces ahead of it. So, P becomes S, O becomes R, S becomes V, I becomes L, T becomes W, and N becomes Q. Then, the letters are revered.

Question 17

Answer = A – CWVWOP

Explanation = Each letter corresponds with the letter two spaces ahead of it. However, the word has been swapped for the 'opposite' season. So, YKPVGT means WINTER. The opposite of SPRING, in this case, is AUTUMN. Applying the rule, this gives us the following: A becomes C, U becomes W, T becomes V, M becomes O, and N becomes P.

Question 18

Answer = B – KMJOZNO

Explanation = Each letter corresponds with the letter 5 spaces behind it. So, P becomes K, R becomes M, O becomes J, T becomes O, E becomes Z, and S becomes N.

Question 19

Answer = B – INTRIGUE

Explanation = Each letter corresponds with the letter 10 spaces ahead of it. So, I becomes S, N becomes X, T becomes D, R becomes B, G becomes Q, U becomes E, and E becomes O.

Question 20

Answer = A – ADMIT

Explanation = Each letter corresponds with the letter 12 spaces ahead of it. So, A becomes M, D becomes P, M becomes Y, I becomes U, and T becomes F.

Question 21

Answer = C – CROWD

Explanation = Each letter corresponds with the letter 2 spaces ahead of it. Then, the word is reversed. So, C becomes E, R becomes T, O becomes Q, W becomes Y, and D becomes F.

Question 22

Answer = B – STEGXKT

Explanation = Each letter corresponds with the letter which is 11 spaces behind it. So, D becomes S, E becomes T, P becomes E, R becomes G, I becomes X, and V becomes K.

Question 23

Answer = D – VAGRAQ

Explanation = Each letter corresponds to the letter 13 spaces ahead of it. So, I becomes V, N becomes A, T becomes G, E becomes R, N becomes A, and D becomes Q.

Question 24

Answer = B – CORRUPT

Explanation = Each letter corresponds to the letter 5 spaces ahead of it. So, C becomes H, O becomes T, R becomes W, U becomes Z, P becomes U, and T becomes Y.

Question 25

Answer = C – SHGDDG

Explanation = Each letter corresponds to the letter 8 spaces behind it. So, A becomes S, P becomes H, O becomes G, and L becomes D.

Question Type 4 - Closest in Meaning

For each question, find the two words that are closest in meaning.

Example:

A	B	C	D	E
Amazed	Indifferent	Awestruck	Considered	Mighty

Answer = A and C.

Explanation = 'Amazed' and 'Awestruck' both mean to be left stunned by an event or occurrence.

Question 1

A	B	C	D	E
Cold	Tepid	Freezing	Warm	Stone

Question 2

A	B	C	D	E
Clear	Warm	Misty	Mild	Foggy

Question 3

A	B	C	D	E
Discard	Save	Preserve	Extinguish	Provide

Question 4

A	B	C	D	E
Phantom	Spirit	Smoke	Howl	Eclipse

Question 5

A	B	C	D	E
Thunder	Precipitation	Electricity	Rumble	Rain

Question 6

A	B	C	D	E
Charm	Oppose	Attract	Divide	Depose

Question 7

A	B	C	D	E
Impress	Guard	Allow	Protect	Detract

Question 8

A	B	C	D	E
Pour	Marinate	Grow	Soak	Dry

Question 9

A	B	C	D	E
Chair	Stick	Seat	Car	Wheel

Question 10

A	B	C	D	E
Desire	Obsess	Propose	Intend	Fixate

Question 11

A	B	C	D	E
Assure	Concern	Worry	Commit	Detain

Question 12

A	B	C	D	E
Deny	Entail	Accept	Coerce	Admit

Question 13

A	B	C	D	E
Spice	Flavour	Fire	Bland	Budge

Question 14

A	B	C	D	E
Solve	Impose	Answer	Interest	Arrive

Question 15

A	B	C	D	E
Begin	Conclude	Continue	End	Prevent

Question 16

A	B	C	D	E
Broth	Burrow	Soup	Burn	Trap

Question 17

A	B	C	D	E
Gown	Trough	Grate	Back	Grille

Question 18

A	B	C	D	E
Expose	Disguise	Destroy	Deligh	Camouflage

Question 19

A	B	C	D	E
Trench	Garden	Pinnacle	Peak	Bind

Question 20

A	B	C	D	E
Blind	Grave	Severe	Dense	Trivial

Question 21

A	B	C	D	E
Sculpture	Batch	Statue	Stone	Pebble

Question 22

A	B	C	D	E
Glow	Haze	Print	Vapour	Mystery

Question 23

A	B	C	D	E
Dust	Fire	Bone	Bite	Sand

Question 24

A	B	C	D	E
House	Church	Office	Police Station	Chapel

Question 25

A	B	C	D	E
Return	Infer	Collect	Lost	Missing

Answers to Question Type 4

Question 1

Answer = A and C

Explanation = Both Cold and Freezing are associated with a low temperature.

Question 2

Answer = C and E

Explanation = Both Misty and Foggy describe weather conditions which obscure vision.

Question 3

Answer = B and C

Explanation = Save and Preserve both mean 'to keep' something.

Question 4

Answer = A and B

Explanation = Phantom and Spirit are both synonyms for 'ghost'.

Question 5

Answer = B and E

Explanation = Rain is a type of Precipitation.

Question 6

Answer = A and C

Explanation = Both Charm and Attract both mean to evoke a positive response from someone else.

Question 7

Answer = B and D

Explanation = Guard and Protect both mean to look after something, or to keep it safe from harm.

Question 8

Answer = B and D

Explanation = Marinate and Soak are both synonyms for 'drench'.

Question 9

Answer = A and C

Explanation = Chair and Seat are both objects that people conventionally sit on.

Question 10

Answer = B and E

Explanation = Obsess and Fixate both mean to completely devote one's attention to something.

Question 11

Answer = B and C

Explanation = Concern and Worry are both synonyms for 'anxiety'.

Question 12

Answer = C and E

Explanation = Both of these words mean to receive something with one's approval.

Question 13

Answer = A and B

Explanation = Spice and Flavour are both words which describe food having a noticeable taste.

Question 14

Answer = A and C

Explanation = Solve and Answer both mean to complete or give a resolution to something.

Question 15

Answer = B and D

Explanation = Both Conclude and End mean the final point of something, or the finishing point.

Question 16

Answer = A and C

Explanation = Broth and Soup are both typically watery dishes.

Question 17

Answer = C and E

Explanation = Grate and Grille are both synonyms for a surface or object with grid-patterns on it.

Question 18

Answer = B and E

Explanation = Both Disguise and Camouflage mean to blend in or hide one's identity or presence.

Question 19

Answer = C and D

Explanation = Both Pinnacle and Peak mean the very top of something, such as a mountain or tower.

Question 20

Answer = B and C

Explanation = Grave and Severe both mean very great or intense, but in a negative way.

Question 21

Answer = A and C

Explanation = Sculpture and Statue are both man-made carvings from a hard substance, such as marble.

Question 22

Answer = B and D

Explanation = Haze and Vapour are both words for thick mist or fog caused by a high density of particles.

Question 23

Answer = A and E

Explanation = Dust and Sand are both fine particles.

Question 24

Answer = B and E

Explanation = Church and Chapel are both buildings with religious connotations.

Question 25

Answer = D and E

Explanation = These words both describe something that cannot be found

Question Type 5 - Hidden Word in the Sentence

For each question, a four-letter word is hidden in the sentence, between two words. These two words are next to each other.

Example:

There was a man enjoying the sun on holiday.

A	B	C	D
There was	man enjoying	the sun	on holiday

Answer = B = 'man enjoying' (mane).

Question 1

The boys were riding their bikes around the roundabout.

A	B	C	D
The boys	were riding	their bikes	the roundabout

Question 2

They had climbed into the attic, but hadn't found anything.

A	B	C	D
They had	climbed into	the attic	hadn't found

Question 3

Nothing had prepared her for the task she would have to complete.

A	B	C	D
Nothing had	prepared her	for the	to complete

Question 4

The situation was quite bad after the hurricane made landfall.

A	B	C	D
The situation	bad after	the hurricane	made landfall

Question 5

They have to take the car to the garage to get the engine fixed.

A	B	C	D
Have to	take the	the garage	engine fixed

Question 6

The absolute control enjoyed by the military dictator was stolen by rebels in the civil war.

A	B	C	D
The absolute	control enjoyed	military dictator	civil war

Question 7

The children thought that everything was ruined. However, they were overreacting.

A	B	C	D
The children	that everything	However, they	were overreacting

Question 8

There was no use trying to explain until everyone had arrived.

A	B	C	D
There was	no use	to explain	until everyone

Question 9

They cleared away his leftover soup, since he wasn't feeling well.

A	B	C	D
They cleared	his leftover	soup since	feeling well

Question 10

The victim explained to the police what had happened to his car.

A	B	C	D
victim explained	the police	what had	happened to

Question 11

There was only a slim elevator to go up to the next floor, so they stood in single file.

A	B	C	D
There was	slim elevator	next floor	single file

Question 12

The emu, seen from afar, came quickly towards them.

A	B	C	D
emu seen	from afar	came quickly	towards them

Question 13

The teams were preparing to achieve their further goal of launching a new programme.

A	B	C	D
The teams	were preparing	achieve their	further goal

Question 14

They discovered that sales of diesel formed only 20% of their income.

A	B	C	D
They discovered	sales of	diesel formed	their income

Question 15

It was odd that the cane stood upright, as if it was alive.

A	B	C	D
It was	odd that	cane stood	was alive

Question 16

The goal post arched and buckled as the children climbed it.

A	B	C	D
The goal	post arched	and buckled	children climbed

Question 17

He knew that her misplaced hat would be around the house.

A	B	C	D
He knew	her misplaced	be around	the house.

Question 18

There was no use in trying to reason with them.

A	B	C	D
There was	no use	in trying	to reason

Question 19

There was a problem: the tape stuck to the carpet and wouldn't come off.

A	B	C	D
a problem	tape stuck	the carpet	wouldn't come

Question 20

There was a glaze staining the glass, making it difficult to see outside.

A	B	C	D
There was	glaze staining	making it	see outside

Question 21

Their grandpa stored lots of old vinyl records in his garage.

A	B	C	D
grandpa stored	lots of	old vinyl	records in

Question 22

They put a plan in place so areas affected could be evacuated quickly.

A	B	C	D
In place	so areas	affected could	evacuated quickly

Question 23

He reckoned that there was a better solution to the problem.

A	B	C	D
He reckoned	that there	better solution	the problem

Question 24

There was no footage of Stacy stealing the laptop.

A	B	C	D
There was	no footage	Stacy stealing	the laptop

Question 25

There was an amused tourist party reading the large sign which read 'DANGER OF DEATH'.

A	B	C	D
An amused	party reading	large sign	danger of

Answers to Question Type 5

Question 1

Answer = D – the roundabout (hero)

Explanation = The boys were riding their bikes around **the ro**undabout.

Question 2

Answer = C – the attic (heat)

Explanation = They had climbed into **the at**tic, but hadn't found anything.

Question 3

Answer = C – for the (fort)

Explanation = Nothing had prepared her **for t**he task she would have to complete.

Question 4

Answer = B – bad after (daft)

Explanation = The situation was quite ba**d aft**er the hurricane made landfall.

Question 5

Answer = A – have to (veto)

Explanation = They ha**ve to** take the car to the garage to get the engine fixed.

Question 6

Answer = B – control enjoyed (role)

Explanation = The absolute cont**rol e**njoyed by the military dictator was stolen by rebels in the civil war.

Question 7

Answer = B – that everything (hate)

Explanation = The children thought t**hat e**verything was ruined. However, they were overreacting.

Question 8

Answer = D – until everyone (tile)

Explanation = There was no use trying to explain un**til e**veryone had arrived.

Question 9

Answer = B – his leftover (isle)

Explanation = They cleared away h**is le**ftover soup, since he wasn't feeling well.

Question 10

Answer = A – victim explained (time)

Explanation = The vic**tim e**xplained to the police what had happened to his car.

Question 11

Answer = B – slim elevator (lime)

Explanation = There was only a s**lim e**levator to go up to the next floor, so they stood in single file.

Question 12

Answer = A – emu seen (muse)

Explanation = The e**mu, se**en from afar, came quickly towards them.

Question 13

Answer = D – further goal (ergo)

Explanation = *The teams were preparing to achieve their furth**er go**al of launching a new programme.*

Question 14

Answer = C – diesel formed (self)

Explanation = They discovered that sales of die**sel f**ormed only 20% of their income.

Question 15

Answer = C – cane stood (nest)

Explanation = It was odd that the ca**ne st**ood upright, as if it was alive.

Question 16

Answer = B – post arched (star)

Explanation = The goal po**st ar**ched and buckled as the children climbed it.

Question 17

Answer = C – be around (bear)

Explanation = He knew that her misplaced hat would **be ar**ound the house somewhere.

Question 18

Answer = D – to reason (tore)

Explanation = There was no use in trying **to re**ason with them.

Question 19

Answer = B – tape stuck (pest)

Explanation = There was a problem: the ta**pe st**uck to the carpet and wouldn't come off.

Question 20

Answer = B – glaze staining (zest)

Explanation = There was a gla**ze st**aining the glass, making it difficult to see outside

Question 21

Answer = A – grandpa stored (past)

Explanation = Their grand**pa st**ored lots of old vinyl records in his garage.

Question 22

Answer = B – so areas (soar)

Explanation = They put a plan in place **so ar**eas affected could be evacuated quickly.

Question 23

Answer = A – He reckoned (here)

Explanation = **He re**ckoned that there was a better solution to the problem.

Question 24

Answer = C – Stacy stealing (cyst)

Explanation = There was no footage of Sta**cy st**ealing the laptop.

Question 25

Answer = B – party reading (tyre)

Explanation = There was an amused tourist par**ty re**ading the large sign which read 'DANGER OF DEATH'.

Question Type 6 - Three Missing Letters

The capitalised word in each question is missing three consecutive letters. Choose the correct consecutive letters from the answer options.

Example:

He ED a lot about getting good grades.

A	B	C	D
PIL	BAR	CAR	VAN

Answer = C = CAR (CARED).

Explanation = "He CARED a lot about getting good grades."

Question 1

They were all CHED up in the corridor.

A	B	C	D
BOT	BUN	PAT	NOT

Question 2

He BEVED that he would make it to the meeting on-time.

A	B	C	D
HOO	REA	LIE	TIE

Question 3

She UNDERSD the consequences of what she was about to do.

A	B	C	D
TIE	TOO	TAN	TAR

Question 4

At the end of the day, the machine was shut down. It had fulfilled its CTION.

A	B	C	D
PUT	ACT	FUN	MAN

Question 5

They all gathered, with protective goggles, to witness the ECSE.

A	B	C	D
LIP	LAP	LIE	LES

Question 6

He had tried so desperately not to SP himself but ended up having too much cake.

A	B	C	D
ELL	OIL	ITE	ARE

Question 7

The TABD newspapers had been particularly ruthless this time.

A	B	C	D
LOT	PAL	LOI	OLD

Question 8

The TOOES had not blended well with the other flavours in the curry.

A	B	C	D
PAN	MAP	MAT	TOM

Question 9

He wanted to protect himself from the sun, but had run out of ION.

A	B	C	D
LAY	TOY	LIE	LOT

Question 10

The songs on the radio just aren't as CHY as they used to be.

A	B	C	D
CAT	DOG	BUY	BAY

Question 11

Sue was extremely SY. She kicked down the door.

A	B	C	D
MOP	GUT	TAD	TIL

Question 12

They had STED too far from the path, and had now become lost.

A	B	C	D
POT	RYE	PUP	RAY

Question 13

There was a ING hole in the attic, and rainwater was flowing through.

A	B	C	D
GAP	TIE	CRY	BOT

Question 14

There was an OVER lack of enthusiasm in the room.

A	B	C	D
JOY	ALL	GUN	OUT

Question 15

ANY could tell that there was a problem with the train's engine; it didn't take an expert to figure that out.

A	B	C	D
SHE	TWO	HER	ONE

Question 16

Not a GLE person in the room volunteered to help.

A	B	C	D
TOP	TUG	SIN	DIE

Question 17

After a PER investigation, it was clear that the burglar had broken in through an air vent.

A	B	C	D
AFT	ROP	TAP	TAN

Question 18

It's important to EN the little things.

A	B	C	D
CRY	JOY	TRY	OIL

Question 19

When the time was right, the army seized ER.

A	B	C	D
POW	LOW	TOW	TIE

Question 20

She was NING for the top spot at the company.

A	B	C	D
TRY	GUN	FRO	GAP

Question 21

All of the DES had to be shut for a week due to snow and ice. No deliveries were made.

A	B	C	D
DEN	PIE	CRY	POT

Question 22

Her job was to DEE any security footage which could be used as evidence for the heist.

A	B	C	D
TON	LET	TAP	ONE

Question 23

Her GES were really high, but this still wasn't enough to secure the job.

A	B	C	D
RAD	RAP	OIL	BAG

Question 24

He called the emergency services. The POL were on their way.

A	B	C	D
ICE	GUY	APP	INK

Question 25

The source of this information was APOPHAL to say the least.

A	B	C	D
CEL	ART	MAT	CRY

Answers to Question Type 6

Question 1

Answer = B - BUN

Explanation = They were all **BUN**CHED up in the corridor.

Question 2

Answer = C - LIE

Explanation = He BE**LIE**VED that he would make it to the meeting

Question 3

Answer = B – TOO

Explanation = She UNDERS**TOO**D the consequences of what she was about to do.

Question 4

Answer = C – FUN

Explanation = At the end of the day, the machine was shut down. It had fulfilled its **FUN**CTION.

Question 5

Answer = A – LIP

Explanation = They all gathered, with protective goggles, to witness the EC**LIP**SE.

Question 6

Answer = B – OIL

Explanation = He had tried so desperately not to SP**OIL** himself but ended up having too much cake.

Question 7

Answer = C – LOI

Explanation = The TAB**LOI**D newspapers had been particularly ruthless this time.

Question 8

Answer = C – MAT

Explanation = The TO**MAT**OES had not blended well with the other flavours in the curry.

Question 9

Answer = D – LOT

Explanation = He wanted to protect himself from the sun, but had run out of **LOT**ION.

Question 10

Answer = A – CAT

Explanation = The songs on the radio just aren't as **CAT**CHY as they used to be.

Question 11

Answer = B – GUT

Explanation = Sue was extremely **GUT**SY. She kicked down the door.

Question 12

Answer = D – RAY

Explanation = They had ST**RAY**ED too far from the path, and had now become lost.

Question 13

Answer = A – GAP

Explanation = There was a **GAP**ING hole in the attic, and rainwater was flowing through.

Question 14

Answer = B – ALL

Explanation = There was an OVER**ALL** lack of enthusiasm in the room.

Question 15

Answer = D – ONE

Explanation = ANY**ONE** could tell that there was a problem with the train's engine; it didn't take an expert to figure that out.

Question 16

Answer = C – SIN

Explanation = Not a **SIN**GLE person in the room volunteered to help.

Question 17

Answer = B – ROP

Explanation = After a P**ROP**ER investigation, it was clear that the burglar had broken in through an air vent.

Question 18

Answer = B – JOY

Explanation = It's important to EN**JOY** the little things.

Question 19

Answer = A – POW

Explanation = When the time was right, they seized **POW**ER.

Question 20

Answer = B – GUN

Explanation = She was **GUN**NING for the top spot at the company.

Question 21

Answer = D – POT

Explanation = All of the DE**POT**S had to be shut for a week due to snow and ice. No deliveries were made.

Question 22

Answer = B – LET

Explanation = Her job was to DE**LET**E any security footage which could be used as evidence for the heist.

Question 23

Answer = A – RAD

Explanation = Her G**RAD**ES were really high, but this still wasn't enough to secure the job.

Question 24

Answer = A – ICE

Explanation = He called the emergency services. The POL**ICE** were on their way.

Question 25

Answer = D – CRY

Explanation = The source of this information was APO**CRY**PHAL to say the least.

Question Type 7 - Letter to Number Codes

In each question, letters stand for specific numbers. Using these numbers, work out the answer to the sum. Remember to use the order of BIDMAS when making calculations.

Example:

A = 1, B = 2, C = 3, D = 4, E = 5

A + D = ?

    A   **B**   **C**   **D**   **E**

Answer = E

Explanation = 1 + 4 = 5.

Question 1

A = 3, B = 10, C = 6, D = 1, E = 9

B − C + A = ?

    A   **B**   **C**   **D**   **E**

Question 2

A = 1, B = 3, C = 5, D = 6, E = 9

B × C − E = ?

    A   **B**   **C**   **D**   **E**

Question 3

A = 4, B = 1, C = 2, D = 5, E = 7

A + C + B = ?

A	B	C	D	E

Question 4

A = 3, B = 4, C = 12, D = 5, E = 1

A × B × E = ?

A	B	C	D	E

Question 5

A = 1, B = 3, C = 10, D = 5, E = 2

C − D − E = ?

A	B	C	D	E

Question 6

A = 5, B = 6, C = 3, D = 2, E = −2

B − D + B = ?

A	B	C	D	E

Question 7

A = 3, B = 2, C = 7, D = 5, E = 8

C + D – A – B = ?

A	B	C	D	E

Question 8

A = 1, B = 2, C = 3, D = 4, E = 5

E – A + C = ?

A	B	C	D	E

Question 9

A = 1, B = 3, C = 5, D = 6, E = 7

B + C – A = ?

A	B	C	D	E

Question 10

A = 1, B = 5, C = 7, D = 10, E = 8

B + D – E = ?

A	B	C	D	E

Question 11

A = 2, B = 1, C = 5, D = 3, E = 4

B + C – D = ?

A　　　　　**B**　　　　　**C**　　　　　**D**　　　　　**E**

Question 12

A = 1, B = 2, C = 3, D = 4, E = 5

E – D = ?

A　　　　　**B**　　　　　**C**　　　　　**D**　　　　　**E**

Question 13

A = 3, B = 5, C = 7, D = 8, E = 2

C + D – B – E – A = ?

A　　　　　**B**　　　　　**C**　　　　　**D**　　　　　**E**

Question 14

A = 1, B = 5, C = 2, D = 4, E = 6

B – C + A = ?

A　　　　　**B**　　　　　**C**　　　　　**D**　　　　　**E**

Question 15

A = 3, B = 1, C = 2, D = 5, E = 12

E – D – C = ?

A	B	C	D	E

Question 16

A = 1, B = 2, C = 3, D = 4, E = 5

D + E – E – B = ?

A	B	C	D	E

Question 17

A = 2, B = 4, C = 6, D = 5, E = 9

A + C + D – B = ?

A	B	C	D	E

Question 18

A = 1, B = 2, C = 5, D = 7, E = 8

E – C – B = ?

A	B	C	D	E

Question 19

A = 4, B = 5, C = 3, D = 1, E = 2

B + C − A = ?

    A   **B**   **C**   **D**   **E**

Question 20

A = 1, B = 2, C = 3, D = 4, E = 7

E − D = ?

    A   **B**   **C**   **D**   **E**

Question 21

A = 3, B = 2, C = 1, D = 5, E = 7

A + B = ?

    A   **B**   **C**   **D**   **E**

Question 22

A = 1, B = 2, C = 5, D = 3, E = 4

A + B + D − A = ?

    A   **B**   **C**   **D**   **E**

Question 23

A = 1, B = 2, C = 3, D = 4, E = 5

B + D – C – A = ?

A	**B**	**C**	**D**	**E**

Question 24

A = 2, B = 3, C = 4, D = 5, E = 6

B + A = ?

A	**B**	**C**	**D**	**E**

Question 25

A = 1, B = 3, C = 8, D = 10, E = 15

B + C – A = ?

A	**B**	**C**	**D**	**E**

Answers to Question Type 7

Question 1

Answer = D

Explanation = 10 − 6 + 3 = 1

Question 2

Answer = D

Explanation = 3 × 5 − 9 = 6

Question 3

Answer = E

Explanation = 4 + 2 + 1 = 7

Question 4

Answer = C

Explanation = 3 × 4 × 1 = 12

Question 5

Answer = B

Explanation = 10 − 5 − 2 = 3

Question 6

Answer = E

Explanation = 6 − 2 + 6 = −2

Question 7

Answer = C

Explanation = $7 + 5 - 3 - 2 = 7$

Question 8

Answer = A

Explanation = $5 - 1 + 3 = 1$

Question 9

Answer = E

Explanation = $3 + 5 - 1 = 7$

Question 10

Answer = C

Explanation = $5 + 10 - 8 = 7$

Question 11

Answer = D

Explanation = $6 + 1 - 3 = 3$

Question 12

Answer = A

Explanation = $5 - 4 = 1$

Question 13

Answer = B

Explanation = $7 + 8 - 2 - 3 - 5 = 5$

Question 14

Answer = C

Explanation = 5 − 2 + 1 = 2

Question 15

Answer = D

Explanation = 12 − 5 − 2 = 5.

Question 16

Answer = B

Explanation = 4 + 5 − 5 − 2 = 2

Question 17

Answer = E

Explanation = 2 + 6 + 5 − 4 = 9

Question 18

Answer = A

Explanation = 8 − 5 − 2 = 1

Question 19

Answer = A

Explanation = 5 + 3 − 4 = 4

Question 20

Answer = C

Explanation = 7 − 4 = 3

Question 21

Answer = D

Explanation = 3 + 2 = 5

Question 22

Answer = C

Explanation = 1 + 2 + 3 − 1 = 5

Question 23

Answer = B

Explanation = 2 + 4 − 3 − 1 = 2

Question 24

Answer = D

Explanation = 3 + 2 = 5

Question 25

Answer = D

Explanation = 3 + 8 − 1 = 10

Question Type 8 - Move the Letter

For each question, there are two words. One letter can be moved from the word on the left to the word on the right, in order to create two new words. Other letters in both words cannot be rearranged.

Example:

Alive   Wake

Answer = Live/Awake.

Explanation = Move 'A' from 'Alive' to create 'Live' and 'Awake'.

Question 1

Pail   Pan

Question 2

Dice   Own

Question 3

Golden   Room

Question 4

Demon   Ever

Question 5

Grown   Gave

[ ]

Question 6

Send   Mite

[ ]

Question 7

Descent   Liver

[ ]

Question 8

String   Cow

[ ]

Question 9

Bold   Rain

[ ]

Question 10

Praying   Moon

[ ]

Question 11

Burly   Pie

[ ]

Question 12

Learn   Gave

Question 13

Provided   Ash

Question 14

Smash   Over

Question 15

Stag   Train

Question 16

Cloud   Lock

Question 17

Scare   Own

Question 18

Sight   Able

Question 19

Front   Done

[ ]

Question 20

Foamy   Arm

[ ]

Question 21

Roam   Range

[ ]

Question 22

Blow   Ink

[ ]

Question 23

Gravel   Ice

[ ]

Question 24

Image   Pant

[ ]

Question 25

Frock   Lax

[ ]

Answers to Question Type 8

Question 1

Answer = Pal / Pain

Explanation = 'I' moves to create 'Pal' and 'Pain'.

Question 2

Answer = Ice / Down

Explanation = 'D' moves to create 'Ice' and 'Down'.

Question 3

Answer = Olden / Groom

Explanation = 'G' moves to create 'Olden' and 'Groom'.

Question 4

Answer = Demo / Never

Explanation = 'N' moves to create 'Demo' and 'Never'.

Question 5

Answer = Gown / Grave

Explanation = 'R' moves to create 'Gown' and 'Grave'.

Question 6

Answer = End / Smite

Explanation = 'S' moves to create 'End' and 'Smite'.

Question 7

Answer = Decent / Sliver

Explanation = 'S' moves to create 'Decent' and 'Sliver'.

Question 8

Answer = Sting / Crow

Explanation = 'R' moves to create 'Sting' and 'Crow'.

Question 9

Answer = Old / Brain

Explanation = 'B' moves to create 'Old' and 'Brain'.

Question 10

Answer = Paying / Moron

Explanation = 'R' moves to create 'Paying' and 'Moron'.

Question 11

Answer = Bury / Pile

Explanation = 'L' moves to create 'Bury' and 'Pile'.

Question 12

Answer = Earn / Gavel

Explanation = 'L' moves to create 'Earn' and 'Gavel'.

Question 13

Answer = Provide / Dash

Explanation = 'D' moves to create 'Provide' and 'Dash'.

Question 14

Answer = Sash / Mover

Explanation = 'M' moves to create 'Sash' and 'Mover'.

Question 15

Answer = Tag / Strain

Explanation = 'S' moves to create 'Tag' and 'Strain'.

Question 16

Answer = Loud / Clock

Explanation = 'C' moves to create 'Loud' and 'Clock'.

Question 17

Answer = Care / Sown

Explanation = 'S' moves to create 'Care' and 'Sown'.

Question 18

Answer = Sigh / Table

Explanation = 'T' moves to create 'Sigh' and 'Table'.

Question 19

Answer = Font / Drone

Explanation = 'R' moves to create 'Font' and 'Drone'.

Question 20

Answer = Foam / Army

Explanation = 'Y' moves to create 'Foam' and 'Army'.

Question 21

Answer = Ram / Orange

Explanation = 'O' moves to create 'Ram' and 'Orange'.

Question 22

Answer = Bow / Link

Explanation = 'L' moves to create 'Bow' and 'Link'.

Question 23

Answer = Grave / Lice

Explanation = 'L' moves to create 'Grave' and 'Lice'.

Question 24

Answer = Mage / Paint

Explanation = 'I' moves to create 'Mage' and 'Paint'.

Question 25

Answer = Rock / Flax

Explanation = 'F' moves to create 'Frock' and 'Lax'.

Question Type 9 - Letter Sequences

For each question, find the pair of letters that complete the sequence. An alphabet is provided to help you.

A B C D E F G H I J K L M N O P Q R S T U V W X Y Z

Example:

AB BC CD DE EF ??

A	B	C	D
IJ	HG	GF	FG

Answer = D = FG.

Explanation = The sequence moves one step forward in the alphabet each time.

Question 1

CG GI IM MO OS ??

A	B	C	D
SV	SW	SU	ST

Question 2

AD EF GJ KL MP ??

A	B	C	D
QR	TU	QT	QS

Question 3

AC DF GI JL MO ??

A	B	C	D
OQ	OP	PR	PQ

A B C D E F G H I J K L M N O P Q R S T U V W X Y Z

Question 4

ZY AC YX CE XW ??

A	B	C	D
XV	EG	XW	CF

Question 5

AZ BX CW DU ET ??

A	B	C	D
FR	FT	GS	FS

Question 6

BA CD FE GH JI ??

A	B	C	D
KJ	JK	KL	LK

Question 7

AC BD EG FH IK ??

A	B	C	D
JK	JL	KL	KM

Question 8

ZY ZX YW YV XU ??

A	B	C	D
WU	XV	XT	WT

A B C D E F G H I J K L M N O P Q R S T U V W X Y Z

Question 9

MN LO KP JQ IR ??

A	B	C	D
HS	GT	HS	HT

Question 10

JK IM HO GQ FS ??

A	B	C	D
EV	ET	EU	ES

Question 11

AC DB EG HF IK ??

A	B	C	D
JL	LJ	MO	LN

Question 12

ZA XY VW TU RS ??

A	B	C	D
QP	PQ	PS	OP

Question 13

AE BF CG DH EI ??

A	B	C	D
FI	IF	FJ	GL

A B C D E F G H I J K L M N O P Q R S T U V W X Y Z

Question 14

AE BH CJ DM EO ??

A	B	C	D
HP	FP	GS	FQ

Question 15

RD TE VF XG ZH ??

A	B	C	D
BI	AB	ZA	IY

Question 16

AA AB AC AD AE ??

A	B	C	D
AZ	AG	AF	BA

Question 17

BZ BY BX BW BV ??

A	B	C	D
BU	BT	AT	AZ

Question 18

AL BM CN DO EP ??

A	B	C	D
FQ	EQ	EN	FP

A B C D E F G H I J K L M N O P Q R S T U V W X Y Z

Question 19

BD ED CD FD DD ??

A	B	C	D
JD	ID	GD	HD

Question 20

AZ BY CZ DY EZ ??

A	B	C	D
GY	EY	FZ	FY

Question 21

AG BG CH DH EI ??

A	B	C	D
FI	FJ	EJ	FF

Question 22

CE EG GI IK KM ??

A	B	C	D
KP	MP	MO	KN

Question 23

QR SR ST UT UV WV ??

A	B	C	D
VX	VW	WV	WX

A B C D E F G H I J K L M N O P Q R S T U V W X Y Z

Question 24

AO OA CU UC YZ ??

A	B	C	D
YZ	ZY	YA	ZA

Question 25

AA BZ CA DZ EA ??

A	B	C	D
EZ	FA	FZ	EG

Answers to Question Type 9

Question 1

Answer = C – SU

Explanation = The pattern is as follows: there is a gap of three letters between the first pair of letters (CG), then a gap of 1 letter between the next two letters (GI). This alternates throughout the sequence as it moves through the alphabet.

Question 2

Answer = A – QR

Explanation = The pattern is as follows. One pair of letters with a two-letter gap between them (AD). Then, the next two consecutive letters (EF). Then, repeat this alternating pattern.

Question 3

Answer = C – PR

Explanation = The pattern is as follows. One pair of letters with a one-letter gap between them (AC). Then, take the next letter (D), and repeat the pattern (DF). This pattern continues as shown.

Question 4

Answer = B – EG

Explanation = The pattern is as follows. Start at the end of the alphabet, with a pair of consecutive letters (ZY). Then, move to the front of the alphabet, and take a pair of letters with a one-letter space between them (AC). Continue this sequence until you reach the answer: EG.

Question 5

Answer = A – FR

Explanation = The pattern is as follows. Each pair takes one letter from the beginning of the alphabet, and one from the end. The first letter is consecutive each time (A, B, C, D, E, F). However, the second letter moves from consecutive, to a one-letter gap (Z, X, W, U, T, R).

Question 6

Answer = C – KL

Explanation = The pattern is as follows. Each pair of letters is consecutive (e.g. BA). However, they alternate between chronological (CD) and reversed (EF). This pattern repeats.

Question 7

Answer = B – JL

Explanation = The pattern is as follows. The first letter in the pair corresponds with another letter 2 spaces ahead (AC, BD). This moves along the alphabet.

Question 8

Answer = C – XT

Explanation = The pattern is as follows. The first letter changes every two stages in the sequence (ZY, ZX, YX). The second letter in the pair moves down once for every step in the sequence.

Question 9

Answer = A – HS

Explanation = The first letter in each pair moves one space towards the beginning of the alphabet on each stage (M, L, K, etc). The second letter in each pair moves one space towards the end of the alphabet on each stage (P, Q, R, etc).

Question 10

Answer = C – EU

Explanation = The first letter in each pair moves one space towards the start of the alphabet (H, G, F). The second letter in each pair moves two spaces towards the end of the alphabet (K, M, O, etc).

Question 11

Answer = B – LJ

Explanation = There is a one-letter gap between the first letter in a pair and the second letter in the pair (AC). However, on every other step, they are reversed (DB). This pattern repeats.

Question 12

Answer = B – PQ

Explanation = The first and second letter in each pair are consecutive (ZA, XY, VW). Then, each pair moves down the alphabet (TU, RS).

Question 13

Answer = C – FJ

Explanation = There is a three-letter gap between the first and second letter of each pair (BF, CG). Then, each pair moves further along in the alphabet (DH, EI).

Question 14

Answer = D – FQ

Explanation = There is a three-letter gap between the two letters in the first pair (HP, CJ). Then, this becomes a five-letter gap, followed by a six-letter gap, and so on. This continues throughout the sequence until we reach an eleven-letter gap (DM, EO).

Question 15

Answer = A – BI

Explanation = The first letter in the pair starts at R, and then moves two spaces along the alphabet to the next letter (TE, VF). The second letter in the pair starts at D, and moves one space along the alphabet to the next letter (XG, ZH).

Question 16

Answer = C – AF

Explanation = The first letter remains the same. The second letter in each pair moves through the alphabet, one space at a time (AA, AB, AC).

Question 17

Answer = A – BU

Explanation = The first letter remains the same. The second letter in each pair moves backwards through the alphabet, one space at a time (BZ, BY, BX).

Question 18

Answer = A – FQ

Explanation = Each pair has a 10-letter gap between the first and second letter (AL, BM). This pair moves one space along the alphabet in each stage of the sequence (CN, DO).

Question 19

Answer = C – GD

Explanation = The second letter in the pair does not change. The first letter alternates between two patterns. On every odd-numbered stage in the sequence, the letter is moving along the alphabet, starting from 'B' (B, C, D). On every even-numbered stage in the sequence, the letter is moving along the alphabet starting from 'E' (E, F, G).

Question 20

Answer = D – FY

Explanation = The first letter in each pair is moving one space along the alphabet (A, B, C, etc). The second letter in each pair alternates between 'Z' and 'Y'.

Question 21

Answer = A – FI

Explanation = The first letter in each pair moves along one space in the alphabet (A, B, C, D, E, etc). The second letter in each pair stays on the same letter for one extra step before moving on (G, G, H, H, I, I).

Question 22

Answer = C – MO

Explanation = There is a one-letter gap between the two letters in each pair (CE, EG, GI). The first letter in each pair is the same as the second letter in the previous pair. This pattern moves along the alphabet (IK, KM).

Question 23

Answer = D – WX

Explanation = The two letters in each pair are consecutive to one another. This moves along the alphabet by one space each time. In every even-numbered step in the sequence, the letters are reversed (e.g. UT instead of TU).

Question 24

Answer = B – ZY

Explanation = Every other pair is a reversed version of the previous pair (e.g. 'AO' and 'OA').

Question 25

Answer = C – FZ

Explanation = The first letter in each pair moves one space along the alphabet (A, B, C, etc). The second letter in each pair alternates between 'A' and 'Z'.

Question Type 10 - Word Relations

For each question, choose two words (one from each pair) that complete the sentence in a way that makes the most sense.

Example:

Asleep is to (awake, principled, aware)

as inside is to (beside, outside, controlled).

Answer = awake/outside

Explanation = These words are opposites. 'Awake' is the opposite of 'asleep', and 'outside' is the opposite of 'inside'.

Question 1

Cold is to (warm wet distant)

as dry is to (laughable pretend soaked).

```


```

Question 2

Bike is to (car vehicle wheel)

as rose is to (flower bright stand).

```


```

Question 3

Error is to (mistake interpretation align)

as barrier is to (bridge fence door).

```


```

Question 4

Relaxed is to (calm stressed composed)

as climb is to (fall between arrive).

[   ]

Question 5

Consider is to (suppose dismiss mock)

as carry is to (meander lift excite).

[   ]

Question 6

Bargain is to (art haggle compensate)

as grapple is to (wrestle hook crash).

[   ]

Question 7

Spider is to (legs eyes hair)

as giraffe is to (feet fur neck).

[   ]

Question 8

Grief is to (ponder mourn perish)

as shock is to (scare smile hide).

[   ]

Question 9

Banshee is to (myth scream dark)

as box is to (cardboard smoke container).

[   ]

Question 10

Distract is to (divert attend adhere)

as behave is to (chant conduct compare).

```



```

Question 11

Behold is to (beware witness arrive)

as reverse is to (similar opposite decide).

```



```

Question 12

Guide is to (demonstrate entail direct)

as careless is to (bounce inconsiderate idle).

```



```

Question 13

Carbon is to (element curve taste)

as plane is to (space aircraft flight).

```



```

Question 14

Accelerate is to (decrease increase decelerate)

as climb is to (pass fall describe).

```



```

Question 15

Sun is to (bright moon rise)

as gold is to (heavy valuable standard).

```



```

Question 16

Trainer is to (boot shoe foot)

as hat is to (head glove warm).

[   ]

Question 17

Bury is to (hide graveyard bathe)

as drink is to (pub station shop).

[   ]

Question 18

Cat is to (mammal tail bark)

as boxer is to (punch tall athlete).

[   ]

Question 19

Bold is to (brave kind alert)

as special is to (similar unique interesting).

[   ]

Question 20

Alleviate is to (provide lessen accept)

as berate is to (help criticise decide).

[   ]

Question 21

Racket is to (commotion tennis belt)

as drill is to (session betray construction).

[   ]

Question 22

Borrow is to (loan bemuse attempt)

as war is to (conflict raw carry).

┌─────────────────┐
│   │
└─────────────────┘

Question 23

Expose is to (cover arrive obtain)

as hold is to (carry drop throw).

┌─────────────────┐
│   │
└─────────────────┘

Question 24

Burglar is to (steal give insert)

as pilot is to (fly drive tell).

┌─────────────────┐
│   │
└─────────────────┘

Question 25

Entry is to (between admission exit)

as accept is to (admit propose scold).

┌─────────────────┐
│   │
└─────────────────┘

Answers to Question Type 10

Question 1

Answer = warm/soaked

Explanation = These words are opposites of one another.

Question 2

Answer = vehicle/flower

Explanation = These are categories. A bike is a type of vehicle, while a rose is a type of flower.

Question 3

Answer = mistake/fence

Explanation = These are synonyms. 'Mistake' is a synonym for error, and 'fence' is a synonym for barrier.

Question 4

Answer = stressed/fall

Explanation = These words are opposites of one another.

Question 5

Answer = suppose/lift

Explanation = These words are synonyms. 'Suppose' is a synonym for consider, and 'lift' is a synonym for carry.

Question 6

Answer = haggle/wrestle

Explanation = These are all synonyms which are also verbs. 'Haggle' and 'bargain' are both related verbs, as are 'grapple' and 'wrestle'.

Question 7

Answer = legs/neck

Explanation = These are both the most defining feature of the two animals. The most defining feature of a spider is its eight legs, and the most defining feature of a giraffe is its long neck.

Question 8

Answer = mourn/scare

Explanation = These words are related verbs. 'Mourn' is a verb related to the noun 'grief', while 'scare' is a verb related to the word 'shock'.

Question 9

Answer = myth/container

Explanation = These are categories. 'Banshee' belongs to the category of 'myth', whilst 'box' belongs to the category of 'container'.

Question 10

Answer = divert/conduct

Explanation = These are synonyms. 'Divert' is a synonym for 'distract', whilst 'conduct' is a synonym for 'behave'.

Question 11

Answer = witness/opposite

Explanation = These are synonyms. 'Witness' is a synonym for 'behold' whilst 'opposite' is a synonym for 'reverse'.

Question 12

Answer = direct/inconsiderate

Explanation = These are synonyms. 'Direct' is a synonym for 'guide' whilst 'inconsiderate' is a synonym for 'careless'.

Question 13

Answer = element/aircraft

Explanation = These are categories. 'Carbon' belongs to the category of 'element', and 'plane' belongs to the category of 'aircraft'.

Question 14

Answer = decelerate/fall

Explanation = These are opposites. 'Decelerate' is the opposite of 'accelerate', and 'fall' is the opposite of 'climb'.

Question 15

Answer = bright/valuable

Explanation = These are both the most defining elements of the related word. The defining element of 'sun' is 'bright', and the defining element of gold is 'valuable'.

Question 16

Answer = foot/head

Explanation = The related term is where the initial term is worn. So, a trainer is worn on the foot, and a hat is worn on the head.

Question 17

Answer = graveyard/pub

Explanation = The related term is a location associated with the verb. 'Bury' is associated with graveyards, and 'drink' is associated with 'pub'.

Question 18

Answer = mammal/athlete

Explanation = These are categories. 'Cat' belongs to the category of 'mammal', whilst 'boxer' belongs to the category of 'athlete'.

Question 19

Answer = brave/unique

Explanation = These are synonyms. 'Brave' is a synonym for 'bold', whilst 'unique' is a synonym for 'special'.

Question 20

Answer = lessen/criticise

Explanation = These are synonyms. 'Lessen' is a synonym for 'alleviate' whilst 'criticise' is a synonym for 'berate'.

Question 21

Answer = tennis/construction

Explanation = The related term is an activity which is associated with the initial term. So, 'racket' is the instrument used in tennis, and a 'drill' is a tool used in construction.

Question 22

Answer = loan/conflict

Explanation = These are synonyms. 'Loan' is a synonym for 'borrow' and 'conflict' is a synonym for war.

Question 23

Answer = cover/drop

Explanation = These words are opposites of one another.

Question 24

Answer = steal/fly

Explanation = These are verbs associated with the initial term. So, burglars steal, and pilots fly.

Question 25

Answer = admission/admit

Explanation = These are synonyms. 'Admission' is a synonym for 'entry', while 'admit' is a synonym for 'accept.

Question Type 11 - Number Sequences

Choose the number which completes the sequence.

Example:

2, 4, 6, 8, 10, ?

A	B	C	D
6	8	12	14

Answer = C = 12.

Explanation = The sequence increases by 2 each time.

Question 1

1, 5, 9, 13, 17, ?

A	B	C	D
20	21	22	19

Question 2

5, 3, 1, -1, -3, ?

A	B	C	D
-5	5	-4	3

Question 3

3, 9, 15, 21, 27, ?

A	B	C	D
30	29	33	32

Question 4

1, 3, 9, 27, 81, ?

A	B	C	D
243	200	195	120

Question 5

500, 250, 125, 62.5, 31.25, ?

A	B	C	D
15.625	18.534	20.2	15.12

Question 6

10, 15, 30, 35, 70, ?

A	B	C	D
90	75	140	280

Question 7

19, 22, 26, 29, 33, ?

A	B	C	D
37	35	34	36

Question 8

7, 14, 28, 56, 112, ?

A	B	C	D
180	140	220	224

Question 9

7, 8, 10, 11, 13, ?

A	B	C	D
13	14	15	16

Question 10

44, 46, 49, 51, 54, ?

A	B	C	D
55	56	57	58

Question 11

11, 25, 39, 53, 67, ?

A	B	C	D
85	79	81	90

Question 12

16, 14, 18, 16, 20, ?

A	B	C	D
18	16	24	22

Question 13

20, 25, 12.5, 17.5, 8.75, ?

A	B	C	D
4.375	5.561	17.5	13.75

Question 14

5, 11, 17, 23, 29, ?

A	B	C	D
36	35	40	33

Question 15

12, 18, 27, 40.5, 60.75, ?

A	B	C	D
101.45	85.4905	91.125	75.25

Question 16

5, 15, 20, 30, 35, ?

A	B	C	D
45	40	50	30

Question 17

3, 10, 17, 24, 31, ?

A	B	C	D
39	40	38	35

Question 18

10, 25, 35, 50, 60, ?

A	B	C	D
85	75	70	80

Question 19

50, 100, 75, 150, 125, ?

A	B	C	D
150	250	225	275

Question 20

5, 8, 11, 14, 17, ?

A	B	C	D
19	21	25	20

Question 21

14, 19, 24, 29, 34, ?

A	B	C	D
39	44	45	40

Question 22

3, 7, 10, 14, 17, ?

A	B	C	D
20	21	23	24

Question 23

15, 20, 27, 32, 39, ?

A	B	C	D
44	47	45	50

Question 24

6, 7, 9, 10, 12, ?

A	B	C	D
15	13	14	17

Question 25

12, 6, 9, 4.5, 7.5, ?

A	B	C	D
15	10.5	3.75	6.5

Answers to Question Type 11

Question 1

Answer = B – 21

Explanation = Add 4 to the current number to get the next one.

Question 2.

Answer = A – –5

Explanation = Minus 2 from the current number to get the next one.

Question 3

Answer = C – 33

Explanation = Add 6 to the current number to get the next one.

Question 4

Answer = A – 243

Explanation = Multiply the current number by 3 to get the next one.

Question 5

Answer = A – 15.625

Explanation = Divide the current number by 2 to get the next one.

Question 6

Answer = B – 75

Explanation = The sequence alternates between add 5, then double. So, 70 + 5 = 75.

Question 7

Answer = D – 36

Explanation = The sequence alternates between add 3, then add 4. So, 33 + 3 = 36.

Question 8

Answer = D – 224

Explanation = Double the current number to get the next one. 112 multiplied by 2 is 224.

Question 9

Answer = B – 14

Explanation = The sequence alternates between add 1 and add 2.

Question 10

Answer = B – 56

Explanation = The sequence alternates between adding 2 and adding 3. So, 54 + 2 = 56.

Question 11

Answer = C – 81

Explanation = Add 14 to the current number to get the next one.

Question 12

Answer = A – 18

Explanation = The sequence alternates between minus 2, and add 4. So, 20 minus 2 is 18.

Question 13

Answer = D – 13.75

Explanation = The sequence alternates between add 5, and divide by 2. So, 8.75 + 5 = 13.75.

Question 14

Answer = B – 35

Explanation = Add 6 to the current number to get the next one.

Question 15

Answer = C – 91.125

Explanation = In this sequence, the next number is the current number + half of the current number. For example, 12 + 6 = 18, and 18 + 9 = 27.

Question 16

Answer = A – 45

Explanation = The sequence alternates between add 10 and add 5. So, 35 + 10 = 45.

Question 17

Answer = C – 38

Explanation = Add 7 to the current number to get the next one.

Question 18

Answer = B – 75

Explanation = The sequence alternates between add 15 and add 10.

Question 19

Answer = B – 250

Explanation = The sequence alternates between multiply by 2 and minus 25. So, 125 multiplied by 2 is 250.

Question 20

Answer = D – 20

Explanation = Add 3 to the current number to get the next one.

Question 21

Answer = A – 39

Explanation = Add 5 to the current number to get the next one.

Question 22

Answer = B – 21

Explanation = The sequence alternates between add 4 and add 3. So, 17 + 4 = 21.

Question 23

Answer = A – 44

Explanation = The sequence alternates between add 5 and add 7. So, 39 + 5 = 44.

Question 24

Answer = B – 13

Explanation = The sequence alternates between add 1 and add 2. So, 12 + 1 = 13.

Question 25

Answer = C – 3.75

Explanation = The sequence alternates between divide by 2, and add 3. So, 7.5 divided by 2 is 3.75.

Question Type 12 - Word Fusion

Choose two words (one from each group) that creates one word. These words cannot be rearranged: the word from the first group must come before the word from the second group.

Example:

(laugh time real) (cold able scary)

Answer = laughable.

Explanation = Combine 'laugh' and 'able' to get the word 'laughable'.

Question 1

(care cook kind) (full less hold)

Question 2

(taste motor tell) (way guide petrol)

Question 3

(bow light brain) (call man irate)

Question 4

(sea rabbit fleet) (pull horse lion)

Question 5

(grave hay husband) (animal yard ham)

Question 6

(shadow feather signal) (axe boxing wave)

```


```

Question 7

(god tail free) (fall top brave)

```


```

Question 8

(cool prior tame) (breath ant pea)

```


```

Question 9

(bile black mucous) (out ice dale)

```


```

Question 10

(tyre camp pack) (site tile terrible)

```


```

Question 11

(coal berate shoe) (entry lace box)

```


```

Question 12

(over under between) (tell told come)

```


```

Question 13

(court crow kind) (box told room)

```


```

Question 14

(god tap tickle) (brake speed hand)

```
[                    ]
```

Question 15

(trap blow bend) (out mend made)

```
[                    ]
```

Question 16

(destroy break tick) (time water tape)

```
[                    ]
```

Question 17

(kind giving care) (giver cool told)

```
[                    ]
```

Question 18

(crow fax tire) (bar bow fore)

```
[                    ]
```

Question 19

(bell blood tack) (bath make craft)

```
[                    ]
```

Question 20

(pile taste track) (less mire deck)

```
[                    ]
```

Question 21

(moon cold sun) (set time bold)

```
[                    ]
```

Question 22

(brick back tame) (bone hold strong)

```
┌─────────────────────┐
│                     │
│                     │
└─────────────────────┘
```

Question 23

(fire pull song) (some fighter exempt)

```
┌─────────────────────┐
│                     │
│                     │
└─────────────────────┘
```

Question 24

(practice bail told) (out fold member)

```
┌─────────────────────┐
│                     │
│                     │
└─────────────────────┘
```

Question 25

(kite buyer board) (trap room punch)

```
┌─────────────────────┐
│                     │
│                     │
└─────────────────────┘
```

Answers to Question Type 12

Question 1

Answer = care/less

Explanation = This creates the word 'careless'.

Question 2

Answer = motor/way

Explanation = This creates the word 'motorway'.

Question 3

Answer = bow/man

Explanation = This creates the word 'bowman'.

Question 4

Answer = sea/horse

Explanation = This creates the word 'seahorse'.

Question 5

Answer = grave/yard

Explanation = This creates the word 'graveyard'.

Question 6

Answer = shadow/boxing

Explanation = This creates the word 'shadowboxing'.

Question 7

Answer = free/fall

Explanation = This creates the word 'freefall'.

Question 8

Answer = cool/ant

Explanation = This creates the word 'coolant'.

Question 9

Answer = black/out

Explanation = This creates the word 'blackout'.

Question 10

Answer = camp/site

Explanation = This creates the word 'campsite'.

Question 11

Answer = shoe/lace

Explanation = This creates the word 'shoelace'.

Question 12

Answer = over/come

Explanation = This creates the word 'overcome'.

Question 13

Answer = court/room

Explanation = This creates the word 'courtroom'.

Question 14

Answer = god/speed

Explanation = This creates the word 'godspeed'.

Question 15

Answer = blow/out

Explanation = This creates the word 'blowout'.

Question 16

Answer = break/water

Explanation = This creates the word 'breakwater'.

Question 17

Answer = care/giver

Explanation = This creates the word 'caregiver'.

Question 18

Answer = crow/bar

Explanation = This creates the word 'crowbar'.

Question 19

Answer = blood/bath

Explanation = This creates the word 'bloodbath'.

Question 20

Answer = taste/less

Explanation = This creates the word 'tasteless'.

Question 21

Answer = sun/set

Explanation = This creates the word 'sunset'.

Question 22

Answer = back/bone

Explanation = This creates the word 'backbone'.

Question 23

Answer = fire/fighter

Explanation = This creates the word 'firefighter'.

Question 24

Answer = bail/out

Explanation = This creates the word 'bailout'.

Question 25

Answer = board/room

Explanation = This creates the word 'boardroom'.

Question Type 13 - Connecting Letters

In the first set of words, the word in the middle is the result of taking letters from the outer two words. Using the same rule, figure out the missing word.

Example:

back (ball) fell

care (?) cell

A	B	C	D
race	call	lera	real

Answer = B = call

Explanation = Take the first and second letters from the first word ('ca') and then the third and fourth letters from the second word ('ll')

Question 1

roam (road) done

bard (?) noon

A	B	C	D
bark	barn	bare	barb

Question 2

ball (fall) turf

burn (?) toot

A	B	C	D
buro	toon	turn	runt

Question 3

bare (tyre) city

fold (?) pogo

A	B	C	D
took	gold	food	good

Question 4

bone (tone) ants

ring (?) bike

A	B	C	D
king	bing	rink	rind

Question 5

dial (diet) fate

bake (?) duel

A	B	C	D
dale	duke	bale	lake

Question 6

polo (peso) aces

goal (?) deal

A	B	C	D
gale	load	lead	gall

Question 7

flee (flea) bath

talk (?) bead

A	B	C	D
kale	tale	balk	bale

Question 8

boom (book) cake

brag (?) fate

A	B	C	D
rage	bare	brat	gate

Question 9

thee (head) clad

icon (?) aide

A	B	C	D
done	cone	code	dine

Question 10

dare (ogre) grow

dose (?) oink

A	B	C	D
sink	nose	does	disk

Question 11

bask (bass) salt

male (?) tell

A	B	C	D
malt	mall	lame	tale

Question 12

dire (dirt) cute

bore (?) cane

A	B	C	D
bone	core	bare	born

Question 13

sale (kale) inky

lost (?) ache

A	B	C	D
host	east	last	hole

Question 14

akin (rain) brag

rein (?) opal

A	B	C	D
pare	pain	naps	maps

Question 15

cold (love) vein

bolt (?) open

A	B	C	D
tool	pent	loop	pelt

Question 16

bask (skid) idle

logo (?) adds

A	B	C	D
gold	load	lads	goad

Question 17

melt (home) halo

mean (?) gala

A	B	C	D
gale	lame	game	name

Question 18

jape (peel) else

ergo (?) reap

A	B	C	D
pare	pear	peer	gore

Question 19

bare (both) moth

told (?) fame

A	B	C	D
fold	tame	melt	dole

Question 20

bury (burn) note

bell (?) tick

A	B	C	D
tell	lick	belt	tile

Question 21

gave (have) echo

sake (?) fate

A	B	C	D
take	tear	sake	seat

Question 22

sell (fall) afar

ammo (?) align

A	B	C	D
limo	bomb	tomb	moat

Question 23

care (cart) path

milk (?) chew

A	B	C	D
chem	lick	mile	khem

Question 24

mark (dark) idle

cold (?) able

A	B	C	D
bold	code	lead	dale

Question 25

male (roam) road

ekes (?) hill

A	B	C	D
kish	hell	isle	hike

Answers to Question Type 13

Question 1

Answer = B – Barn

Explanation = Take the first three letters from the first word (ROA, BAR) and the first letter from the second word (D, N).

Question 2

Answer = C – Turn

Explanation = Take the final letter from the second word (F, T) and the final three letters from the first word (ALL, URN).

Question 3

Answer = B – Gold

Explanation = Take the final two letters from the second word (TY, GO), and the final two letters from the first word (RE, LD).

Question 4

Answer = A – King

Explanation = Take the third letter from the second word (T, K), and the final three letters from the first word (ONE, ING).

Question 5

Answer = C – Bale

Explanation = Take the final two letters from the second word and swap them around (TE becomes ET, EL becomes LE). Then, add them to the first two letters from the first word (DI, BA).

Question 6

Answer = D – Gall

Explanation = Take the final two letters from the second word (ES, AL) and the first and final letter from the first word (PO, GL).

Question 7

Answer = B – Tale

Explanation = Take the first three letters from the first word (TAL). Then, take the second letter from the second word (E).

Question 8

Answer = C – Brat

Explanation = Take the third letter from the second word (B), and the first three letters from the first word (RAT).

Question 9

Answer = C – Code

Explanation = Take the second and third letters from the first word (CO), and the third and fourth letters from the second word (DE).

Question 10

Answer = B – Nose

Explanation = Take the third letter from the second word (N). Then, take the first letter from the second word (O). Then, take the final 2 letters from the first word (SE).

Question 11

Answer = A – Malt

Explanation = Take the first three letters from the first word (MAL). Then, take the first letter from the second word (T).

Question 12

Answer = D – Born

Explanation = Take the first three letters from the first word (BOR). Then, take the third letter from the second word (N).

Question 13

Answer = A – Host

Explanation = Take the third letter from the second word (H). Then, take the second, third, and fourth letters of the first word (OST).

Question 14

Answer = B – Pain

Explanation = Take the second and third letters from the second word (PA), and the third and fourth letters of the first word (IN).

Question 15

Answer = C – Loop

Explanation = Take the second and third letters from the first word (OL), and then swap them around (OL becomes LO) and then take the first two letters from the second word (OP).

Question 16

Answer = D – Goad

Explanation = Take the third and fourth letters from the first word (GO). Then, take the first and second words from the second word (AD).

Question 17

Answer = C – Game

Explanation = Take the first and final letters from the second word (GA). Then, take the first and second letters from the first word (ME).

Question 18

Answer = D – Gore

Explanation = Take the third and fourth letters from the first word (GO). Then, take the first and second letters from the second word (RE).

Question 19

Answer = B – Tame

Explanation = Take the first letter from the first word (T). Then, take the second, third, and fourth letters from the second word (AME).

Question 20

Answer = C – Belt

Explanation = Take the first three letters from the first word (BEL), and then take the first letter from the second word (T).

Question 21

Answer = A – Take

Explanation = Take the third letter from the second word (T). Then, take the second, third, and fourth letters from the first word (AKE).

Question 22

Answer = A – Limo

Explanation = Take the second and third letters from the second word (LI). Then, take the third and fourth letters from the first word (MO).

Question 23

Answer = C – Mile

Explanation = Take the first three letters from the first word (MIL). Then, take the third letter from the second word (O).

Question 24

Answer = A – Bold

Explanation = First, take the second letter from the second word (B). Then, take the second, third, and fourth letters from the first word (OLD).

Question 25

Answer = D – Hike

Explanation = Take the first and second letters from the second word (HI). Then, take the first and second letters from the first word (EK), but reverse them (e.g. MO becomes OM).

Question Type 14 - Connecting Letters

Find the pair of letters that makes the most sense in the context of the other letters. An alphabet is provided to help you.

A B C D E F G H I J K L M N O P Q R S T U V W X Y Z

Example:

AB is to CD

as FG is to (??)

A	B	C	D
IH	HI	GH	JI

Answer = B = HI.

Explanation = The second set of letters begins straight after the end of the second set. So, FG becomes HI.

Question 1

BC is to TT

as GH is to (??)

A	B	C	D
XX	YY	ZZ	ZA

Question 2

LO is to MN

as GJ is to (??)

A	B	C	D
HI	GH	IJ	IK

Question 3

PQ is to TS

as AB is to (??)

A	B	C	D
DE	CD	ED	DC

A B C D E F G H I J K L M N O P Q R S T U V W X Y Z

Question 4

AD is to EF

as FI is to (??)

A	B	C	D
IJ	JK	JL	HJ

Question 5

DD is to FF

as RR is to (??)

A	B	C	D
QQ	UU	TT	WW

Question 6

BC is to AW

as CD is to (??)

A	B	C	D
DD	CX	BY	BX

Question 7

EF is to HH

as OP is to (??)

A	B	C	D
RR	QQ	TT	UU

Question 8

AB is to YY

As BC is to (??)

A	B	C	D
XX	AA	ZZ	CC

A B C D E F G H I J K L M N O P Q R S T U V W X Y Z

Question 9

CC is to EF

as DD is to (??)

A	B	C	D
GH	EF	FG	HI

Question 10

NO is to XY

as EF is to (??)

A	B	C	D
PQ	NO	PO	OP

Question 11

AA is to ZZ

as YY is to (??)

A	B	C	D
CC	XX	WW	BB

Question 12

DF is to CE

as GI is to (??)

A	B	C	D
FH	GJ	CD	HI

Question 13

EF is to MN

as DE is to (??)

A	B	C	D
PQ	KL	IJ	LM

A B C D E F G H I J K L M N O P Q R S T U V W X Y Z

Question 14

BB is to FF

as JJ is to (??)

A	B	C	D
MM	OO	NN	LL

Question 15

AZ is to BY

as CX is to (??)

A	B	C	D
VD	WD	EW	DW

Question 16

CC is to GH

as RR is to (??)

A	B	C	D
WV	VW	WT	UV

Question 17

VV is to RR

as FF is to (??)

A	B	C	D
DD	CC	BB	AA

Question 18

AD is to UX

as CF is to (??)

A	B	C	D
UX	WY	WZ	TV

A B C D E F G H I J K L M N O P Q R S T U V W X Y Z

Question 19

BB is to GH

as DD is to (??)

A	B	C	D
IJ	JI	HI	JK

Question 20

ON is to DC

as SR is to (??)

A	B	C	D
HI	MN	GH	HG

Question 21

LM is to VW

as CD is to (??)

A	B	C	D
ON	LD	LK	MN

Question 22

UV is to AB

as XY is to (??)

A	B	C	D
FE	GF	DE	PO

Question 23

ST is to PQ

GH is to (??)

A	B	C	D
DE	JK	MN	IH

A B C D E F G H I J K L M N O P Q R S T U V W X Y Z

Question 24

QP is to RS

as DC is to (??)

A	B	C	D
FG	FE	EF	GH

Question 25

NN is to EE

as YY is to (??)

A	B	C	D
OO	NN	QQ	PP

Answers to Question Type 14

Question 1

Answer = B – YY

Explanation = There is a seventeen-letter gap between the second letter in the first pair and the second pair of letters.

Question 2

Answer = A – HI

Explanation = The second pair of letters are the two letters between the letters in the first pair.

Question 3

Answer = C – ED

Explanation = There is a one-letter gap between the first pair of letters and the second pair of letters. The letters are in alphabetical order in the first pair, but are reversed in the second pair (ST becomes TS, DE becomes ED).

Question 4

Answer = B – JK

Explanation = The two letters in the second pair come directly after the final letter in the first pair.

Question 5

Answer = C – TT

Explanation = There is a one-letter gap between the first pair of letters and the second pair of letters.

Question 6

Answer = D – BX

Explanation = There is a 22-letter gap between the two letters in the second pair. The first letter of the second pair is the letter directly before the first letter of the first pair (e.g. A comes before B, and B comes before C).

Question 7

Answer = A – RR

Explanation = There is a one-letter gap between the second letter in the first pair and the second pair.

Question 8

Answer = C – ZZ

Explanation = If each letter in the alphabet is assigned a number from 1 to 26, then the letter in the second pair is 23 greater than the second letter in the first pair.

Question 9

Answer = C – FG

Explanation = There is a 1-letter gap between the first pair of letters, and the first letter of the second pair of letters.

Question 10

Answer = D – OP

Explanation = If each letter is assigned a number from 1 to 26, then the second pair of letters are 10 greater than the first pair (e.g. 14 and 15 is to 24 and 25).

Question 11

Answer = B – XX

Explanation = The second pair of letters comes before the first pair of letters.

Question 12

Answer = A – FH

Explanation = The first letter in the second pair comes before the first letter in the first pair. The second letter in the second pair comes before the second letter in the first pair.

Question 13

Answer = D – LM

Explanation = If each letter in the alphabet is assigned a number from 1 to 26, the second pair of letters are 8 higher than the first pair.

Question 14

Answer = C – NN

Explanation = There is a four-letter gap between the first pair of letters and the second pair of letters.

Question 15

Answer = D – DW

Explanation = The first letter moves one space forward in the alphabet, whilst the second letter moves one space back in the alphabet.

Question 16

Answer = B – VW

Explanation = There is a three-letter gap between the first pair of letters and the second pair of letters.

Question 17

Answer = C – BB

Explanation = There is a three-letter gap between the first pair of letters and the second pair of letters.

Question 18

Answer = C – WZ

Explanation = There is a two-letter gap between the letters in each pair. If each letter is assigned a number from 1 to 26, then the second pair of letters are 20 greater than the first pair.

Question 19

Answer = A – IJ

Explanation = There is a four-letter gap between the first pair of letters and the second pair of letters.

Question 20

Answer = D – HG

Explanation = If each letter is assigned a number from 1 to 26, then the second pair of letters are 11 less than the first pair.

Question 21

Answer = D – MN

Explanation = If each letter is assigned a number from 1 to 26, then the second pair of letters has a value 10 higher than the first pair (12 and 13 is to 22 and 23).

Question 22

Answer = C – DE

Explanation = If each letter is assigned a number from 1 to 26, then the second pair of letters are 20 less than the first pair.

Question 23

Answer = A – DE

Explanation = There is a one-letter gap between the first pair of letters and the second pair of letters.

Question 24

Answer = C – EF

Explanation = The first pair of letters are in reverse order (e.g. QP instead of PQ). The second pair of letters are chronological to the first letter in the first pair.

Question 25

Answer = D – PP

Explanation = If each letter is assigned a number from 1 to 26, then the second letter is 9 less than the first letter (e.g. N = 14 and E = 5).

Question Type 15 - Opposite Meanings (One From Each Group)

Choose two words, one from each group, that are the most opposite in their meanings.

Example:

(debt, take, pay) (give, accept, share)

Answer = Take/Give.

Explanation = 'Give' is the opposite of 'take'.

Question 1

(evil, justice, jury) (bad, rude, hero)

Question 2

(release, kill, beat) (sad, arrest, prison)

Question 3

(yawn, plentiful, blood) (empty, black, red)

Question 4

(punch, shave, toilet) (wave, yellow, stroke)

Question 5

(slow, fiction, relish) (despair, lick, ambiguous)

Question 6

(green, primary, toilet) (blue, yellow, secondary)

Question 7

(Laura, dry, pants) (water, silk, David)

Question 8

(perfume, lake, earth) (Henry, Yugoslavia, sky)

Question 9

(particular, soil, bench) (benevolent, sallow, indiscriminate)

Question 10

(wasp, football, fictional) (reality, rugby, saint)

Question 11

(lie, broken, fool) (professor, honest, martyr)

Question 12

(Claire, joyful, buddy) (Nigel, penfriend, adversary)

Question 13

(Africa, continent, micro) (Asia, gargantuan, lollipop)

Question 14

(rules, park, buck) (laws, pool, doe)

Question 15

(read, angel, poem) (fantasy, write, Satan)

Question 16

(skill, scrumptious, crumpet) (pudding, luck, roulette)

Question 17

(imposter, flagrant, robbery) (genuine, article, laidback)

Question 18

(Christmas, filthy, merry) (animal, common, spotless)

Question 19

(happy, sad, year) (new, smooch, distraught)

Question 20

(jaundice, rabbit, fresh) (stepladder, stale, mould)

Question 21

(asparagus, orange, pattern) (sapphire, plain, smelly)

Question 22

(pen, Louise, filth) (Kenneth, soap, fence)

Question 23

(wart, master, jester) (idiot, slave, query)

Question 24

(grass, elephant, gun) (peace, prosperity, chapel)

Question 25

(sanctuary, opulent, sacrilegious) (ruby, pretentious, derelict)

Answers to Question Type 15

Question 1

Answer = evil, hero

Explanation = Evil and hero are the two words which have the most opposite meaning. Evil is defined as being 'wicked and immoral' whereas hero means, roughly speaking, the opposite of this.

Question 2

Answer = release, arrest

Explanation = Release and arrest are the two words which have the most opposite meaning. Both of them are verbs. Release means 'to free, or unburden' whereas arresting someone has the opposite effect.

Question 3

Answer = plentiful, empty

Explanation = Plentiful and empty are the two words which have the most opposite meaning. Plentiful means to be full of something, or that there is a great deal of something. Empty means that there is nothing.

Question 4

Answer = punch, stroke

Explanation = Punch and stroke are the two words which have the most opposite meaning. Both are verbs, but punch means to strike or hit, whereas stroke is a gentle act, of endearment.

Question 5

Answer = relish, despair

Explanation = Relish and despair are the two words which have the most opposite meaning. Relish means to enjoy or savour something. Despair means to lose hope, or become disheartened.

Question 6

Answer = primary, secondary

Explanation = Primary and secondary are the two words which have the most opposite meaning. Primary is defined by being 'the first' whereas secondary is 'the second'.

Question 7

Answer = dry, water

Explanation = Dry and water are the two words which have the most opposite meaning. Water is wet, which is the opposite of dry.

Question 8

Answer = earth, sky

Explanation = Earth and sky are the two words which have the most opposite meaning. Earth is directly below us, on the ground, whereas sky is above us, in the air.

Question 9

Answer = particular, indiscriminate

Explanation = Particular and indiscriminate are the two words which have the most opposite meaning. To be particular means to be selective about something, whereas being indiscriminate is the opposite of this.

Question 10

Answer = fictional, reality

Explanation = Fictional and reality are the two words which have the most opposite meaning. Fictional means 'made up' or 'imagined'. Reality is the word used to describe non-fictional, or real life, events.

Question 11

Answer = lie, honest

Explanation = Lie and honest are the two words which have the most opposite meaning. If you lie, you are not honest, and vice versa.

Question 12

Answer = buddy, adversary

Explanation = Buddy and adversary are the two words which have the most opposite meaning. The term buddy is a slang term meaning friend, used to refer to someone whom you know and like. The word adversary is another term for enemy or opponent.

Question 13

Answer = micro, gargantuan

Explanation = Micro and gargantuan are the two words which have the most opposite meaning. Micro means tiny, or very small, and gargantuan means very large or enormous.

Question 14

Answer = buck, doe

Explanation = Buck and doe are the two words which have the most opposite meaning. Buck is the name for a male deer, whereas doe is the word used for a female deer.

Question 15

Answer = angel, Satan

Explanation = Angel and Satan are the two words which have the most opposite meaning. Angels are typically associated with heaven, whereas Satan is associated with hell.

Question 16

Answer = skill, luck

Explanation = Skill and luck are the two words which have the most opposite meaning. If you achieve something via luck, then you have not used skill, and vice versa.

Question 17

Answer = imposter, genuine

Explanation = Imposter and genuine are the two words which have the most opposite meaning. An imposter is something that is false, or a pretence. The word genuine is the opposite of this, and means 'real'.

Question 18

Answer = filthy, spotless

Explanation = Filthy and spotless are the two words which have the most opposite meaning. Filthy means 'dirty' or 'unclean' and spotless is the opposite to this.

Question 19

Answer = happy, distraught

Explanation = Happy and distraught are the two words which have the most opposite meaning. Happy means being elated or full of joy. Distraught is the opposite.

Question 20

Answer = fresh, stale

Explanation = Fresh and stale are the two words which have the most opposite meaning. Fresh means new or recent and stale is the term for something that has existed for a long time, or expired.

Question 21

Answer = pattern, plain

Explanation = Pattern and plain are the two words which have the most opposite meaning. A pattern is an intricate design, whereas if something is plain then it has no intricate design qualities.

Question 22

Answer = filth, soap

Explanation = Filth and soap are the two words which have the most opposite meaning. Filth means to be very dirty or unclean, whereas soap is a device that you use to become clean.

Question 23

Answer = master, slave

Explanation = Master and slave are the two words which have the most opposite meaning. Master means 'lord', and is a term used to refer to someone who is in control. Slave means 'underling' or someone who is given commands.

Question 24

Answer = gun, peace

Explanation = Gun and peace are the two words which have the most opposite meaning. A gun is a tool of war and violence, whereas peace is the opposite of war and violence.

Question 25

Answer = opulent, derelict

Explanation = Opulent and derelict are the two words which have the most opposite meaning. When something is opulent it is rich and full of grandeur. Derelict means the opposite of this.

Question Type 16 - Completing the Sum

Choose the number which will result in a correct sum.

Example:

4 + 9 = 15 − (?)

A	B	C	D
2	1	3	5

Answer = A = 2.

Explanation = 4 + 9 = 13. 15 − 2 = 13.

Question 1

17 + 4 = 19 + (?)

A	B	C	D
1	3	2	5

Question 2

5 + 8 = 3 + (?)

A	B	C	D
13	8	10	9

Question 3

29 + 12 = 49 − (?)

A	B	C	D
8	9	12	7

Question 4

16 × 2 = 29 + (?)

A	B	C	D
5	4	2	3

Question 5

$10 + 15 = 5 \times (?)$

A	B	C	D
5	25	7	9

Question 6

$45 + 4 = 7 \times (?)$

A	B	C	D
6	7	9	8

Question 7

$19 - 5 = 6 + (?)$

A	B	C	D
7	4	6	8

Question 8

$10 + 16 = 30 - (?)$

A	B	C	D
1	6	4	5

Question 9

$17 + 8 = 50 \div (?)$

A	B	C	D
2	4	6	7

Question 10

$15 + 6 = 3 \times (?)$

A	B	C	D
6	7	8	9

Question 11

$14 \times 2 = (?) + 20$

A	B	C	D
7	6	8	10

Question 12

$9 \times 5 = 56 - (?)$

A	B	C	D
15	13	9	11

Question 13

$13 + 8 = 15 + (?)$

A	B	C	D
6	10	12	11

Question 14

$10 + 8 = 18 + (?)$

A	B	C	D
2	1	0	4

Question 15

$7 + 4 + 3 = 22 - (?)$

A	B	C	D
7	8	9	10

Question 16

$9 + 2 = 19 - (?)$

A	B	C	D
9	7	6	8

Question 17

17 × 2 = 102 ÷ (?)

A	B	C	D
5	3	4	2

Question 18

59 + 5 = 8 × (?)

A	B	C	D
4	6	9	8

Question 19

77 + 5 = 56 + (?)

A	B	C	D
30	24	26	34

Question 20

66 ÷ 6 = (?) + 5

A	B	C	D
6	5	7	8

Question 21

43 + 7 = 200 ÷ (?)

A	B	C	D
5	2	3	4

Question 22

65 + 8 = 80 − (?)

A	B	C	D
8	7	5	3

Question 23

21 + 7 = 40 − (?)

A	B	C	D
10	14	13	12

Question 24

17 + 5 = 2 × (?)

A	B	C	D
11	12	10	13

Question 25

56 + 20 = 4 × (?)

A	B	C	D
21	19	24	18

Answers to Question Type 16

Question 1

Answer = C – 2

Explanation = 17 + 4 = 21, 21 − 19 = 2.

Question 2

Answer = C – 10

Explanation = 5 + 8 = 13, 13 − 3 = 10.

Question 3

Answer = A – 8

Explanation = 29 + 12 = 41, 41 + 8 = 49.

Question 4

Answer = D – 3

Explanation = 16 × 2 = 32, 32 − 29 = 3.

Question 5

Answer = A – 5

Explanation = 10 + 15 = 25, 5 × 5 = 25.

Question 6

Answer = B – 7

Explanation = 45 + 4 = 49, 7 × 7 = 49.

Question 7

Answer = D – 8

Explanation = 19 − 5 = 14, 6 + 8 = 14.

Question 8

Answer = C – 4

Explanation = 10 + 16 = 26, 30 – 4 = 26.

Question 9

Answer = A – 2

Explanation = 17 + 8 = 25, 50 ÷ 2 = 25.

Question 10

Answer = B – 7

Explanation = 15 + 6 = 21, 3 × 7 = 21.

Question 11

Answer = C – 8

Explanation = 14 × 2 = 28, 20 + 8 = 28.

Question 12

Answer = D – 11

Explanation = 9 × 5 = 45, 56 – 45 = 11.

Question 13

Answer = A – 6

Explanation = 13 + 8 = 21, 15 + 6 = 21.

Question 14

Answer = C – 0

Explanation = 10 + 8 = 18, 18 + 0 = 18.

Question 15

Answer = B – 22

Explanation = 7 + 4 + 3 = 14, 22 – 14 = 8.

Question 16

Answer = D – 8

Explanation = 9 + 2 = 11, 19 – 8 = 11.

Question 17

Answer = B – 3

Explanation = 17 × 2 = 34, 102 ÷ 3 = 34.

Question 18

Answer = D – 8

Explanation = 59 + 5 = 64, 8 × 8 = 64.

Question 19

Answer = C – 26

Explanation = 77 + 5 = 82, 56 + 26 = 82.

Question 20

Answer = A – 6

Explanation = 66 ÷ 6 = 11, 5 + 6 = 11.

Question 21

Answer = D – 4

Explanation = 43 + 7 = 50, 200 ÷ 4 = 50.

Question 22

Answer = B – 7

Explanation = 65 + 8 = 73, 80 – 7 = 73.

Question 23

Answer = D – 12

Explanation = 21 + 7 = 28, 40 – 12 = 28.

Question 24

Answer = A – 11

Explanation = 17 + 5 = 22, 2 × 11 = 22.

Question 25

Answer = B – 19

Explanation = 56 + 20 = 76, 4 × 19 = 76.

Question Type 17 - Number Relations

For each question, there are two sets of numbers. The middle number relates to the numbers either side of it. The relationship between the three numbers is the same in both sets.

Example:

(2 [5] 7) (8 [12] 20) (6 [?] 15)

A	B	C	D
5	6	8	9

Answer = D = 9

Explanation = 15 − 6 = 9.

Question 1

(7 [2] 5) (15 [8] 7) (22 [?] 10]

A	B	C	D
32	8	12	16

Question 2

(6 [18] 3) (2 [6] 3) (5 [?] 3)

A	B	C	D
15	12	14	2

Question 3

(5 [8] 3) (5 [9] 4) (5 [?] 12)

A	B	C	D
14	15	17	10

Question 4

(6 [24] 4) (4 [36] 9) (6 [?] 3)

A	B	C	D
21	9	16	18

Question 5

(15 [21] 6) (21 [29] 8) (12 [?] 9)

A	B	C	D
3	19	21	17

Question 6

(15 [25] 10) (20 [56] 36) (6 [?] 30)

A	B	C	D
36	24	28	40

Question 7

(10 [6] 4) (7 [6] 1) (9 [?] 4)

A	B	C	D
6	5	4	3

Question 8

(10 [19] 9) (12 [19] 7) (14 [?] 9)

A	B	C	D
7	22	18	23

Question 9

(60 [54] 6) (44 [30] 14) (55 [?] 13)

A	B	C	D
42	44	47	68

Question 10

(25 [51] 26) (20 (41) 21) (23 [?] 26)

A	B	C	D
51	49	47	50

Question 11

(10 [4] 6) (7 [1] 6) (18 [?] 8)

A	B	C	D
26	12	10	24

Question 12

(8 [16] 2) (5 [25] 5) (8 [?] 3)

A	B	C	D
32	11	24	36

Question 13

(60 [20] 3) (8 [2] 4) (30 [?] 5)

A	B	C	D
6	5	3	7

Question 14

(15 [30] 15) (20 [24] 4) (7 [?] 14)

A	B	C	D
12	24	7	21

Question 15

(21 [28] 7) (15 [37] 22) (35 [?] 7)

A	B	C	D
45	28	42	49

Question 16

(7 [7] 49) (5 [5] 25) (3 [?] 21)

A	B	C	D
8	10	7	63

Question 17

(6 [60] 54) (5 [21] 16) (7 [?] 44)

A	B	C	D
51	50	53	52

Question 18

(18 [6] 12) (66 [61] 5) (8 [?] 3)

A	B	C	D
3	5	24	30

Question 19

(8 [50] 42) (10 [40] 30) (8 [?] 40)

A	B	C	D
30	48	32	24

Question 20

(6 [15] 9) (5 [12] 7) (9 [?] 8)

A	B	C	D
20	18	16	17

Question 21

(4 [16] 4) (2 [28] 14) (15 [?] 3)

A	B	C	D
45	5	30	18

Question 22

(90 [6] 84) (55 [50] 5) (4 [?] 3)

A	B	C	D
1	12	4	3

Question 23

(9 [81] 9) (4 [40] 10) (21 [?] 3)

A	B	C	D
18	24	42	63

Question 24

(12 [24] 12) (6 [16] 10) (8 [?] 15)

A	B	C	D
120	23	25	30

Question 25

(8 [7] 1) (15 [4] 11) (18 [?] 10)

A	B	C	D
10	7	8	5

Answers to Question Type 17

Question 1

Answer = C – 12

Explanation = The middle number equals the first number minus the second number (e.g. 7 – 5 = 2). 22 – 10 = 12.

Question 2

Answer = A – 15

Explanation = The middle number is the result of multiplying the other two numbers together (e.g. 6 × 3 = 18). 5 × 3 = 15.

Question 3

Answer = C – 17

Explanation = The middle number is the result of adding the two other numbers together. 5 + 12 = 17.

Question 4

Answer = D – 18

Explanation = The middle number is the result of multiplying the two other numbers together. 6 × 3 = 18.

Question 5

Answer = C – 21

Explanation = The middle number is the result of adding the two other numbers together. 12 + 9 = 21.

Question 6

Answer = A – 36

Explanation = The middle number is the result of adding the two other numbers together. 6 + 30 = 36.

Question 7

Answer = B – 5

Explanation = The middle number is the result of subtracting the second number from the first number. 9 – 4 = 5.

Question 8

Answer = D – 23

Explanation = The middle number is the result of adding the two other numbers together. 14 + 9 = 23.

Question 9

Answer = A – 42

Explanation = The middle number is the result of subtracting the second number from the first number. 55 – 13 = 42.

Question 10

Answer = B – 49

Explanation = The middle number is the result of adding the two other numbers together. 23 + 26 = 49.

Question 11

Answer = C – 10

Explanation = The middle number is the result of subtracting the second number from the first number. 18 – 8 = 10.

Question 12

Answer = C – 24

Explanation = The middle number is the result of multiplying the other two numbers together. 8 × 3 = 24.

Question 13

Answer = A – 6

Explanation = The middle number is the result of dividing the first number by the second number. 30 ÷ 5 = 6.

Question 14

Answer = D – 21

Explanation = The middle number is the result of adding the other two numbers together. 7 + 14 = 21.

Question 15

Answer = C – 42

Explanation = The middle number is the result of adding the other two numbers together. 35 + 7 = 42.

Question 16

Answer = C – 7

Explanation = The middle number is the result of dividing the second number by the first number. 21 ÷ 3 = 7.

Question 17

Answer = A – 51

Explanation = The middle number is the result of adding the other two numbers together. 7 + 44 = 51.

Question 18

Answer = B – 5

Explanation = The middle number is the result of subtracting the second number from the first number. 8 – 3 = 5.

Question 19

Answer = B – 48

Explanation = The middle number is the result of adding the other two numbers together. 8 + 40 = 48.

Question 20

Answer = D – 17

Explanation = The middle number is the result of adding the other two numbers together. 9 + 8 = 17.

Question 21

Answer = A – 45

Explanation = The middle number is the result of multiplying the other two numbers. 15 × 3 = 45.

Question 22

Answer = A – 1

Explanation = The middle number is the result of subtracting the second number from the first. 4 – 3 = 1.

Question 23

Answer = D – 63

Explanation = The middle number is the result of multiplying the other two numbers. 21 × 3 = 63.

Question 24

Answer = B – 23

Explanation = The middle number is the result of adding the other two numbers together. 8 + 15 = 23.

Question 25

Answer = C – 8

Explanation = The middle number is the result of subtracting the second number from the first number. 18 – 10 = 8.

Question Type 18 - Number/Word Codes

For each question, there are four words. You have been provided a code for three of the four words. However, the codes are not written in the same order as the words. Using the codes, figure out the correct code for each question.

Example:

BARK BANE BACK BONE

1293 1263 1254

What is the code for BAKE?

A	B	C	D
1623	1234	1362	4125

Answer = B = 1234

Explanation = B = 1, A = 2, K = 3, E = 4.

Question 1

PEEK PEEL LEAK LEER

8443 8442 3412

What is the code for LAKE?

A	B	C	D
3248	3142	3124	8142

Question 2

TELL LAKE TONE TOLL

5233 3467 5287

What is the code for TAKE?

A	B	C	D
3478	7843	7423	5467

Question 3

DOOR REED DEAR READ

4221 1334 1254

What is the code for DARE?

A	B	C	D
1542	1354	1543	1452

Question 4

BALE BULB BULL TALL

2536 1533 2433

What is the code for TALE?

A	B	C	D
1532	1536	2433	6321

Question 5

LAME MELT TELL LEAN

3511 1265 6513

What is the code for MEAL?

A	B	C	D
3521	6532	3124	6521

Question 6

POOL LOOP POLE LEAP

2147 2557 7521

What is the code for PALE?

A	B	C	D
7541	7412	7421	2175

Question 7

COOL TOOL LOOT COLT

4231 4223 1223

What is the code for TOLL?

A	B	C	D
3221	1433	1422	1233

Question 8

BILL PILL PILE LIPS

3156 3155 2155

What is the code for BELL?

A	B	C	D
2633	2611	2655	2155

Question 9

LONE TONE TOON NOON

2662 1662 1623

What is the code for NOTE?

A	B	C	D
3621	2633	2613	6231

Question 10

KISS SICK KICK HOLD

5749 8122 2138

What is the code for LICK?

A	B	C	D
2148	4138	2128	4148

Question 11

BASK LESS LETS MAST

4322 7625 1382

What is the code for ABLE?

A	B	C	D
4312	7642	1324	6743

Question 12

CORE ROPE COPE CAPE

1635 1245 4235

What is the code for PEAR?

A	B	C	D
3624	3564	3164	1634

Question 13

BARE CARE CANE BEEN

1445 1234 6234

What is the code for NEAR?

A	B	C	D
5431	6214	5432	5423

Question 14

MOLE MALE LOOM LOAM

6231 1365 6221

What is the code for ALMA?

A	B	C	D
3613	1615	3623	1626

Question 15

DOOM MOOD MODE HOME

1552 2513 4523

What is the code for HOOD?

A	B	C	D
4552	4551	2441	3554

Question 16

LOOT LOTS SOOT TOOL

1623 1662 2661

What is the code for LOST?

A	B	C	D
3612	1361	1362	1632

Question 17

BAKE BIKE BILE LAKE

1234 6234 1564

What is the code for BALE?

A	B	C	D
1264	1234	1564	6254

Question 18

TILE MILE TILT MIME

6521 4521 4541

What is the code for TIME?

A	B	C	D
6541	6521	4561	6425

Question 19

FILL LIFT LIFE LEFT

3514 1233 3215

What is the code for FELT?

A	B	C	D
3244	1324	1524	1534

Question 20

WANT WAND DART TART

5135 8125 7135

What is the code for WARD?

A	B	C	D
8173	8135	8137	8127

Question 21

HEAL FEAT FEET BEAT

5663 7623 5623

What is the code for BEET?

A	B	C	D
7553	7663	5662	2663

Question 22

READ REAR REED BEAR

5446 1435 5435

What is the code for BEAD?

A	B	C	D
1436	1543	4613	1465

Question 23

HELL HILT TILT HILL

3123 5622 5123

What is the code for TELL?

A	B	C	D
5622	2533	3511	3622

Question 24

IDEA IDLE DEED LEAD

8732 7227 3217

What is the code for LAID?

A	B	C	D
2387	3287	3187	8732

Question 25

COAL COOL LOAD CODE

1263 1224 4256

What is the code for DEAL?

A	B	C	D
4263	6453	6354	6214

Answers to Question Type 18

Question 1

Answer = C – 3124

Explanation = L = 3, A = 1, K = 2, E = 4.

Question 2

Answer = D – 5467

Explanation = T = 5, A = 4, K = 6, E = 7.

Question 3

Answer = A – 1542

Explanation = D = 1, A = 5, R = 4, E = 2.

Question 4

Answer = B – 1536

Explanation = T = 1, A = 5, L = 3, E = 6.

Question 5

Answer = D – 6521

Explanation = M = 6, E = 5, A = 2, L = 1.

Question 6

Answer = C – 7421

Explanation = P = 7, A = 4, L = 2, E = 1.

Question 7

Answer = D – 1233

Explanation = T = 1, O = 2, L = 3.

Question 8

Answer = C – 2655

Explanation = B = 2, E = 6, L = 5.

Question 9

Answer = C – 2613

Explanation = N = 2, O = 6, T = 1, E = 3.

Question 10

Answer = B – 4138

Explanation = L = 4, I = 1, C = 3, K = 8.

Question 11

Answer = D – 6743

Explanation = A = 6, B = 7, L = 4, E = 3.

Question 12

Answer = B – 3564

Explanation = P = 3, E = 5, A = 6, R = 4.

Question 13

Answer = D – 5423

Explanation = N = 4, E = 4, A = 2, R = 3.

Question 14

Answer = A – 3613

Explanation = A = 3, L = 6, M = 1.

Question 15

Answer = B – 4551

Explanation = H = 4, O = 5, D = 1.

Question 16

Answer = D – 1632

Explanation = L = 1, O = 6, S = 3, T = 2.

Question 17

Answer = A – 1264

Explanation = B = 1, A = 2, L = 6, E = 4.

Question 18

Answer = A – 6541

Explanation = T = 6, I = 5, M = 4, E = 1.

Question 19

Answer = D – 1534

Explanation = F = 1, E = 5, L = 3, T = 4

Question 20

Answer = C – 8137

Explanation = W = 7, A = 8, N = 4, T = 9.

Question 21

Answer = B – 7663

Explanation = B = 7, E = 6, T = 3.

Question 22

Answer = A – 1436

Explanation = B = 1, E = 4, A = 3, D = 6.

Question 23

Answer = D – 3622

Explanation = T = 3, E = 6, L = 2.

Question 24

Answer = C – 3187

Explanation = L = 3, A = 1, I = 8, D = 7.

Question 25

Answer = C – 6354

Explanation = D = 6, E = 3, A = 5, L = 4.

Question Type 19 - Complete the Word

For each question, find the word that completes the third set of words in the same way that the first two pairs are related.

Example: flower (low) crowd (row) canter (?)

Answer = ant

Explanation = Take the second, third, and fourth letters to get 'ant'.

Question 1

brute (but) glute (gut) trend (?)

Question 2

tonne (one) bruin (run) prism (?)

Question 3

fight (fig) gunner (gun) sonic (?)

Question 4

glider (lie) grain (ran) orange (?)

Question 5

lower (owe) champ (ham) brown (?)

Question 6

glove (log) drive (rid) black (?)

| |
| |

Question 7

grime (gem) lotto (lot) fauna (?)

| |
| |

Question 8

layer (aye) atone (ton) erode (?)

| |
| |

Question 9

satin (sin) basin (bin) begun (?)

| |
| |

Question 10

trove (vet) promo (mop) dunno (?)

| |
| |

Question 11

steal (let) items (set) steep (?)

| |
| |

Question 12

stale (eat) stump (put) inurn (?)

```
[                    ]
```

Question 13

adore (red) gneta (tan) waver (?)

```
[                    ]
```

Question 14

brave (bar) olive (oil) froth (?)

```
[                    ]
```

Question 15

grass (sag) naifs (fin) props (?)

```
[                    ]
```

Question 16

caper (ape) other (the) brand (?)

```
[                    ]
```

Question 17

broth (rob) carry (arc) plonk (?)

```
[                    ]
```

Question 18

atoll (lot) keyed (dye) spill (?)

┌─────────────────────────┐
│   │
│   │
└─────────────────────────┘

Question 19

bring (bin) teary (tar) brags (?)

┌─────────────────────────┐
│   │
│   │
└─────────────────────────┘

Question 20

broke (ore) tithe (tie) debug (?)

┌─────────────────────────┐
│   │
│   │
└─────────────────────────┘

Question 21

pagan (pan) befog (bog) dixie (?)

┌─────────────────────────┐
│   │
│   │
└─────────────────────────┘

Question 22

baits (tab) pangs (gap) nifty (?)

┌─────────────────────────┐
│   │
│   │
└─────────────────────────┘

Question 23

doing (dog) beast (bet) yeast (?)

┌─────────────────────────┐
│   │
│   │
└─────────────────────────┘

Question 24

oxide (ode) throe (toe) greet (?)

Question 25

robot (bot) angel (gel) robin (?)

Answers to Question Type 19

Question 1

Answer = ten

Explanation = Take the first, third, and fourth letters.

Question 2

Answer = rim

Explanation = Take the second, third, and fifth letters.

Question 3

Answer = son

Explanation = Take the first three letters.

Question 4

Answer = rag

Explanation = Take the second letter, the third letter, and the fifth letter.

Question 5

Answer = row

Explanation = Take the second, third, and fourth letters.

Question 6

Answer = lab

Explanation = Take the second, third, and first letters.

Question 7

Answer = fan

Explanation = Take the first, fifth, and fourth letters.

Question 8

Answer = rod

Explanation = Take the second, third, and fourth letters.

Question 9

Answer = bun

Explanation = Take the first, fourth, and fifth letters.

Question 10

Answer = nod

Explanation = Take the fourth, fifth, and first letters.

Question 11

Answer = pet

Explanation = Take the fifth, third, and second letters.

Question 12

Answer = nun

Explanation = Take the fifth, third, and second letters.

Question 13

Answer = era

Explanation = Take the fourth, fifth, and second letters.

Question 14

Answer = for

Explanation = Take the first, third, and second letters.

Question 15

Answer = pop

Explanation = Take the fourth, third, and first letters.

Question 16

Answer = ran

Explanation = Take the second, third, and fourth letters.

Question 17

Answer = lop

Explanation = Take the second, third, and first letters.

Question 18

Answer = lip

Explanation = Take the fifth, third, and second letters.

Question 19

Answer = bag

Explanation = Take the first, third, and fourth letters.

Question 20

Answer = beg

Explanation = Take the third, second, and fifth letters.

Question 21

Answer = die

Explanation = Take the first, fourth, and fifth letters.

Question 22

Answer = tin

Explanation = Take the fourth, second, and first letters.

Question 23

Answer = yet

Explanation = Take the first, second, and fifth letters.

Question 24

Answer = get

Explanation = Take the first, fourth, and fifth letters.

Question 25

Answer = bin

Explanation = Take the third, fourth, and fifth letters.

Question Type 20 - Find the Same Meaning

Choose the word which suits both of the pairs of other words.

Example:

(Courageous, Heroic) (Vivid, Clear)

Tired	Enraged	Bold	Lucid

Answer = Bold

Explanation = 'Bold' is a synonym for 'heroic' and 'vivid'.

Question 1

(Unsympathetic, Blunt) (Winter, Snow)

Cold	Hot	Brown	Snail

Question 2

(Wave, Swim) (Fish, Shark)

Pond	Hand	Sea	Foot

Question 3

(Punch, Fist) (Bowling, Baseball)

Tuna	Strike	Catfish	Cheese

Question 4

(Basin, Cutlery) (Drown, Dive)

Ocean	Cat	Sink	Tennis

Question 5

(Fake, Pretend) (Penicillin, Injection)

Grass	Pen	Ballpoint	Doctor

Question 6

(Power Watt) (Ram, Assault)

Punching   Kicking   Battery   Boxing

Question 7

(Verdict, Decision) (Write, Grammar)

Punctuate   Sentence   Destroy   Annihilate

Question 8

(Safe, Steady) (Hay, Jodhpurs)

Chickens   Stable   Farm   Sky

Question 9

(Iris, Retina) (Study, Learn)

Soldier   Ballad   Retriever   Pupil

Question 10

(Birth, Appear) (Scheme, Plan)

Basket   Uterus   Cauliflower   Hatch

Question 11

(Excess, Superfluous) (Save, Mercy)

Murder   Grin   Carpet   Spare

Question 12

(Combine, Merge) (Dive, Float)

Lake   Pool   Gasp   Sigh

Question 13

(Chase, Tease) (Perform, Act)

Play	Movie	Library	Shout

Question 14

(Spell, Cast) (Professional, Teacher)

Wand	Sword	Handgun	Staff

Question 15

(Plan, Template) (Select, Pick)

Draft	Delete	Terminate	Show

Question 16

(Stand, Ascend) (Petal, Stem)

Gravitate	Nucleus	Float	Rose

Question 17

(Sleep, Dormant) (Devious, Falsities)

Fraud	Charlatan	Embezzler	Lies

Question 18

(Nasal, Dust) (Putt, Chip)

Lake	Flour	Bogey	Interview

Question 19

(Helpful, Thoughtful) (Species, Race)

Naive	Universal	Kind	Considerate

Question 20

(Trek, Climb) (Piano, Keys)

Leap	Scale	Vertices	Graze

Question 21

(Pair, Join) (Flame, Stick)

Timber	Steel	Pipe	Match

Question 22

(Explode, Atom) (Dive, Pool)

Plank	Bomb	Plane	Body

Question 23

(Escape, Avoid) (Nimble, Rodent)

Pupil	Prefect	Weasel	Headmaster

Question 24

(Flame, Prod) (Chip, Ante)

Fork	Hammer	Poker	Shaun

Question 25

(Clothes, Board) (Bronze, Stone)

Pacific	Jurassic	Apes	Iron

Answers to Question Type 20

Question 1

Answer = Cold

Explanation = If someone is unsympathetic or blunt they could also be seen as acting in a cold manner. Likewise, 'winter' and 'snow' are both associated with cold, in terms of weather.

Question 2

Answer = Sea

Explanation = Waves and swimming are associated with the sea. The sea is also where you will find fish and sharks.

Question 3

Answer = Strike

Explanation = Both punch and fist are closely associated with striking someone. In bowling, players aim to score a strike. In baseball, the players are given three chances, or strikes.

Question 4

Answer = Sink

Explanation = A basin is also known as a sink, and a sink is where you wash up cutlery. Sinking is also commonly associated with drowning, and diving into water.

Question 5

Answer = Doctor

Explanation = The term doctor is not just a name given for a medical professional, which links with penicillin and injections. Doctor is another word for committing fraudulent activity.

Question 6

Answer = Battery

Explanation = The terms power and watt are associated with electricity, which links with batteries – used to supply power to electronic devices. Battery is also the name for a violent action, such as assault, or ramming something.

Question 7

Answer = Sentence

Explanation = To sentence someone, in legal terms, is to reach a decision or verdict on their legal status. Writing and grammar are also associated with literary sentences.

Question 8

Answer = Stable

Explanation = The term stable can mean safe or steady, i.e. in a fixed or balanced manner. It is also the name for a horse's home, in which you will find hay, and jodhpurs (riding boots).

Question 9

Answer = Pupil

Explanation = The pupil forms a part of the eye, as does the iris and the retina. Likewise, pupils at school study and learn.

Question 10

Answer = Hatch

Explanation = Hatching, in animals born from eggs, relates to birth and the time when they first appear in the world. Hatch can also mean to scheme or plan, for example, 'I hatched a clever plan.'

Question 11

Answer = Spare

Explanation = Excess or superfluous relate to 'having too much', or spare. The term spare is also used to describe the act of 'refraining from harming someone'.

Question 12

Answer = Pool

Explanation = The terms combine and merge can refer to 'pooling' something together, or adding things to one group. Likewise, you would dive or float in a (swimming) pool.

Question 13

Answer = Play

Explanation = Chasing or teasing are both acts associated with playing. In a dramatic play, actors perform or act.

Question 14

Answer = Staff

Explanation = In fantastical terms, a staff is used to cast spells. A professional person, or a teacher, could be considered a member of staff.

Question 15

Answer = Draft

Explanation = A template or plan is a term used for an early form of work, which is missing something (the same as a draft). In sports, a draft is where players are selected or picked.

Question 16

Answer = Rose

Explanation = To stand or ascend is to rise (past tense rose). A petal and stem are both parts associated with a flower, such as a rose.

Question 17

Answer = Lies

Explanation = A person who is sleeping or dormant will generally be lying down. If you are devious or spreading falsities, then you are telling lies.

Question 18

Answer = Bogey

Explanation = A bogey is a term used to describe a piece of dried nasal mucus, which is used to stop dust getting into the nose. Bogey is also associated with golf, as is putting and chipping.

Question 19

Answer = Kind

Explanation = Being kind is another term for being helpful or thoughtful. Kind can also be used in the context of 'type' or 'sort', which can be associated with species or race.

Question 20

Answer = Scale

Explanation = To scale something means climbing it, also associated with trekking. In musical terms, a scale is closely related with pianos and keys.

Question 21

Answer = Match

Explanation = To match something is to join it, or pair it. Match can also refer to matchsticks, which create a flame.

Question 22

Answer = Bomb

Explanation = A bomb explodes, and nuclear bombs are also known as atom bombs. One popular form of diving, into a swimming pool, is known as bombing.

Question 23

Answer = Weasel

Explanation = Weasels are generally very fast and hard to catch, and they are a form of rodent. The term 'weasel' can also mean escaping or avoiding. I.e. 'To weasel your way out of something.'

Question 24

Answer = Poker

Explanation = In order to increase the size of a fireplace flame, you would prod at the wood with a poker. Both chip and ante are terms associated with the card game.

Question 25

Answer = Iron

Explanation = Clothes and board are associated with ironing board. Bronze and Stone are names of ages in early British history, and link with the Iron Age.

A FEW FINAL WORDS...

Congratulations on reaching the end of the workbook. Before we leave you, we want to provide you with some details about what your results mean and how an employer will use them to assess you for the position you are applying for.

WHAT IS A GOOD SCORE?

It is difficult to pinpoint what constitutes a good score. The reason for this is because the majority of employers will use your scores in the verbal reasoning test in conjunction with your scores from any other element of assessment/ testing. In addition to sitting a verbal reasoning test you will most probably be required to sit other testing elements such as a numerical reasoning test, a group exercise and an interview.

The assessor/employer will also compare your test marks against those who have previously sat the test. This is often referred to as a comparison group. It is now more common for an assessor to grade your scores in the test compared to the previous comparison group, as opposed to giving you a definitive score. For example, you could be graded as follows:

Your scores are well above average compared to previous test takers in this category.

Your scores are above average compared to previous test takers in this category.

Your scores are in the average range for those who have previously sat this test.

Your scores are below average compared to previous test takers in this category.

If you have obtained above average scores during the final mock exam you are certainly on the way to gaining a good score in your actual test.

Thank you for choosing How2Become as your source of help and preparation for your verbal reasoning tests. Good luck with all your future tests and career moves.

TAKE A LOOK AT OUR OTHER REASONING GUIDES!

Each guide is packed full of examples and practice questions, to ensure that you make the most out of your revision time and can aim to achieve 100%!

FOR MORE INFORMATION ON OUR TESTING GUIDES, PLEASE CHECK OUT THE FOLLOWING:

WWW.HOW2BECOME.COM.

Get Access To

FREE

Verbal Reasoning Test Questions

www.MyPsychometricTests.co.uk

Printed in Great Britain
by Amazon